Recent Research in Psychology

J. Richard Eiser

The Expression of Attitude

Springer-Verlag
New York Berlin Heidelberg
London Paris Tokyo

J. Richard Eiser
Department of Psychology
Washington Singer Laboratories
University of Exeter
Exeter, England EX4 4QG

With 3 Illustrations

Library of Congress Cataloging in Publication Data
Eiser, J. Richard.
  The expression of attitude.
  (Recent research in psychology)
  Bibliography: p.
  1. Attitude (Psychology)   2. Expression.
3. Judgment.   4. Learning, Psychology of.
I. Title. II. Series. [DNLM: 1. Attitude.
2. Judgment.   3. Learning.   BF 441 E363e]
BF327.E37   1987   152.4'52   87-13062

Printed and bound by Edwards Brothers, Ann Arbor, Michigan.
Printed in the United States of America.

9 8 7 6 5 4 3 2 1

ISBN 0-387-96562-9 Springer-Verlag New York Berlin Heidelberg
ISBN 3-540-96562-9 Springer-Verlag Berlin Heidelberg New York

CONTENTS

I. A summary of the argument

In the following pages, I shall attempt to consider a number of very broad and interrelated questions: what are attitudes, how do they relate to behavior, how are they acquired, and in what ways can they be shared? Basic to this attempt is the argument that consistency, within attitude structure and between attitudes and behavior, arises primarily from the influence of interpersonal rather than intrapersonal processes. Reliance is put on three main bodies of theory — those of the psychology of learning, the psychology of judgment, and the notion of accountability.

Both learning and judgment principles predict consistency across response modalities to specific stimuli within a defined frame of reference. However verbal attitude statements may be learnt under different conditions from those under which affective and goal-orientated responses to attitude objects are acquired. Pressures to bring verbal attitude statements in particular into line with other attitude-relevant responses are social in origin, and depend on individuals learning how they will be held accountable by others for what they say and do. Accountability in turn depends on the imposition of frames of reference in terms of which separate situations and responses are categorized together.

Such frames of reference are often communicated through language that selectively emphasizes salient criteria for the evaluation of events and behavior. There are many factors that can influence the relative salience of different criteria for evaluation but one of the most important will be compatibility of particular criteria with the communicator's personal attitude. Attitudes may thus come to be shared to the extent that individuals acquire specific attitude-relevant behaviors under similar conditions, and to the extent that they learn to account for such behaviors in terms of similar evaluative frames of reference. However, one cannot necessarily infer consensual forms of thought and experience from consensual forms of talk. Whereas attitudes and attitudinal consistency are social products, individual differences in attitudes persist, and cannot be defined away by attempting to equate attitudes with 'social representations'.

Even so, one of the main shortcomings of many attitude theories is their emphasis on individualistic, intrapsychic factors to the relative neglect of the social and communicative context within which attitudes are acquired and expressed. Not only the expression but also the experience of attitude is shaped by how we have learnt to anticipate others' interpretations of what we say and do. For this reason, attitude is both a subjective experience and a social product, and the expression of attitude is a social act.

II. Attitude as the meaning of expressive behavior

Different definitions of attitude demonstrate the basic issue that attitude research has failed to resolve — that of the relationship between feelings and inner experiences on the one hand and observable behavior on the other. Operationally, attitudes are almost always defined in terms of responses to some object along a bipolar evaluative dimension. Such operationalism, however, does nothing to explain what psychologists try to do with the concept of attitude, and this, predominantly, is to predict and explain behavior. Allport's (1935) definition of attitude as "a mental and neural state of readiness" makes this more motivational sense explicit.

Social psychological research on 'attitude-behavior relations' has fallen into a familiar mould. Researchers have gone around measuring evaluative responses, and interpreting them as indicators of subjective experiences capable of motivating behavior. They have then measured observable behavior (other than the verbal reports on which the attitude measure is based), and calculated correlations. Where such correlations have been satisfactory, they have been interpreted as reflecting causality; where they have been unsatisfactory, they have been described as signs of an 'attitude-behavior discrepancy'.

A few years ago (Eiser, 1980), I proposed that much traditional attitude research has encountered difficulties by assuming
that the relationship of attitudes to behavior is causal rather
than logical. My argument at the time started by drawing on the
logical distinction between sense and reference, pointing out
that attitude statements (e.g. "That rose is beautiful") may
presuppose that people have inner experiences, but do not refer
to these experiences. Instead refer to objects or events in the
external world that elicit such experiences. Understanding what
kinds of inner experiences may be expressed by such a statement
is part of understanding the statement itself — however, it is
the object, not the experience, that is described. The same
would go for 'non-attitudinal' descriptive statements such as
"That rose is red". We may be less able to establish the truth-
value of attitude statements than that of other descriptions of
the external world, but that does not stop people often being
extremely offended (and in some contexts, even to the death) when
others disagree with their attitudes on an important issue. But
if attitude statements referred to separate, individual, private
experiences, where would be the contradiction in different people
holding different attitudes? The fact that attitudinal disagreements may be difficult to resolve does not alter the fact that
they are perceived as disagreements.

The problem is very much one of steering a middle course
between the extremes of positivism and mentalism. A definition
of attitude as, say, a set of verbal responses, may sound all
very scientific and empirical, but it leaves out the absolutely
crucial fact that we understand such verbal responses as
meaningful — and as meaningful in a distinctive kind of way.

4

Attitudes therefore are not mere verbal responses, but the subjective evaluation experiences that are communicated through various channels but particularly through language. At the same time, it is insufficient to define attitudes as subjective evaluative experience if we avoid the issue of how experience is communicated, and rendered public. This is why it is vital to recognize that attitudes are not just experiences, but experiences of objects with a public reference.

I therefore went on to propose that attitude should be regarded as the meaning of a person's expressive behavior, arguing that the relationship of attitudes to expressive behavior seems

> ..."to be essentially a logical one, analogous to the relation between meaning and utterance. We need to assume that words have meaning to understand verbal behaviour, but we do not need to regard the meaning of the word as something which has an independent existence, nor as a distinct entity which causes the verbal behaviour. Just as words have meaning, people have attitudes, and the concept of attitude is no less important for understanding human social behaviour than is the concept of meaning for understanding language (Eiser, 1980, p.19)".

From this definition, I went on to draw two related implications. The one was concerned with measurement and was essentially a reiteration of the familiar argument (e.g. Thurstone, 1928) that the measurement of attitudes in terms of a single evaluative scale may be pragmatically justified but is still an oversimplification:

> "If the only important distinctions within such expressive behaviour were ones that could be completely dealt with in

5

terms of a single continuum ranging from overall positive to overall negative affect, we could all communicate our attitudes perfectly adequately through a combination of gurgles, grunts and growls, without any need for language (Eiser, 1980, p.53)".

The other implication related to work on the 'attitude-behavior discrepancy'. Here I accepted the Fishbein and Ajzen (1975) emphasis on the importance of matching levels of generality - specificity:

"The 'attitude-behavior discrepancy' is essentially an artefact of the haphazard selection of specific behavioral indices which researchers have tried to relate to general measures of attitudes. If the selection of specific verbal indices (for inclusion in an attitude scale) were as lax and arbitrary, we would quickly have a situation in which we had to talk of an 'attitude-attitude discrepancy': attitudes would not simply fail to predict behaviour, they would have to be considered self-contradictory even at the level of verbal expression (Eiser, 1980, p.52)".

On re-reading these passages, I now recognize a number of ambiguities that need to be resolved. Working back through the argument, I would now accept that it may indeed be quite usual for people to be "self-contradictory even at the level of verbal behaviour", so long as others, including psychologists, allow them to be so. Consistency may be something imposed through social interaction, rather than a natural state of cognitive homeostasis. Next, I would also accept that "gurgles, grunts, and growls", and such like, may still reflect feelings that may sometimes have important relations to other behavior. The major ambiguities however, are with the phrase 'the meaning of expressive behavior'.

The difficulties with the proposal definition are not insuperable, but they are fundamental: what is meant by 'meaning', and what by 'expressive behaviour'?

The term _meaning_ combines different usages. On the one hand, the meaning of words, (and longer linguistic structures) is defined according to an agreed (or imposed) social convention, that may indeed change over time but not simply on the whim of a single individual. In other words, 'meaning' is a _social product_ of agreed conventions of communication. Because of these conventions, the meaning of an expressive act may be thought of as what could be legitimately understood by a _listener_ or observer of such an act.

On the other hand, the term 'meaning' can be used to reflect _intent_, as in "I didn't mean to do that". From this point of view, 'meaning' again becomes something to which a person performing an expressive act may be thought to have privileged access. It is difficult to keep these two senses entirely distinct (consider, for instance, the French "veuillir dire") and the reason may be partly that speech is typically reacted to as though it is intentional. However, having said that, there is a difference between calling an act intentional, and regarding it as motivated by a specific intention (Anscombe, 1963), and there is a further difference between claiming that intentional expressive acts 'have meaning', and saying that the meaning of any such act _is_ the intention associated with it. My position now is that I would not want to incorporate such assumptions about intentionality into my use of the term 'meaning' in this context, and I would not wish to identify meaning with intention.

The difficulty with the term 'expressive behavior' is one of setting the category boundaries. Clearly I wished in my earlier statement to set these wider than mere language, but beyond that I was unspecific. But this, of course, is the core issue in attitude—behavior research (albeit in a different guise to usual) — what kinds of behavior are to be taken as expressive of attitude and what kinds are not? Different behaviors may be interpreted as more or less 'expressive', depending on the context, so a mere listing of 'expressive' and 'non—expressive' behaviors would be a vain enterprise.

Reliance on the notion of intentionalipy, furthermore, does not resolve the difficulty. We may make different inferences from behavior, depending on whether or not we regard it as intentional, but I would not want to assume that behavior can only be regarded as expressive if it reflects a deliberate intention to communicate. Instead, I shall adopt the position that the decision to regard a piece of behavior as 'expressive' depends primarily on its interpretability within its context in terms of socially accepted codes, and that this interpretability depends, in large part, on its apparent consistency. The point is that expressive behavior, in this context, does not consist simply of the performance of acts that happen to be interpretable by others, or that happen to allow others to infer something about one's private feelings and experience. Rather, expressive behavior is performed in such a way as to be perceived and understood by others. Thus the expression of attitude is a social act that presupposes an audience by whom that expression may be understood. The manner in which the presence, size and composition of the audience can influence how people express their attitudes, is an empirical question, and one that has been the focus of much research over the years. What is more important

8

for the present argument is the fact that the social context of attitude expression implies rules or codes for such expression. It is because of these rules that meaningful expression can be distinguished from production of meaningless sounds, and indeed that one can decide whether what is being expressed is in fact an attitude. After all, 'expressive behavior' may express other experiences than attitudinal ones, so that a definition of attitude cannot avoid dealing with the distinguishing features of attitudes as opposed to other kinds of thoughts or feelings. If, however, we regard attitude as _evaluative_ experience, then the link to expressive behavior is more easily discerned: the kind of behavior we can regard as meaningfully expressive of attitude will be behavior that communicates an _evaluation_ of the attitude object.

If this line of argument is followed, the emphasis shifts to the question of how people interpret behavior as expressive of attitude, and what they demand of such behavior before they treat it as decodable in a particular way. The question of How do people acquire attitudes? then needs to be rephrased as How do people acquire the behaviors that are interpreted as expressive of attitudes? This is the question which I shall now consider before returning to the question of how such behaviors are inter—preted.

III. Attitude-relevant behavior and the 'three-component' view

     I do not wish to impose a restrictive definition on the
kinds of behavior that are to be seen as attitude-relevant, but
the following broad classification may be useful:

1) Emotional or affective reactions. Although many theorists
have regarded affect as the key component of attitude, affective
reactions may be difficult to measure directly. Researchers have
typically relied, therefore, on linguistic expressions of affect
(see below). However, attention has been paid to physiological
arousal as an effect and mediator of manipulations of cognitive
dissonance (Cooper & Fazio, 1984; Cooper, Zanna & Taves, 1978;
Fazio, Zanna and Cooper, 1977).

2) Adaptive or goal-directed action. Here one is dealing potentially with any behavior (perceived as) instrumental to the
achievement of some goal (Ginsburg, Brenner & von Cranach, 1985;
von Cranach, Kalbermatten, Indemuehle & Gugler, 1982). In general, though, such behavior may be distinguished from:

3) Linguistic behavior (including the use of any arbitrary
communication code other than language). Most attitude research
has taken linguistic behavior as the prime indicator of attitude,
whether in the form of naturally occurring statements, or of

10

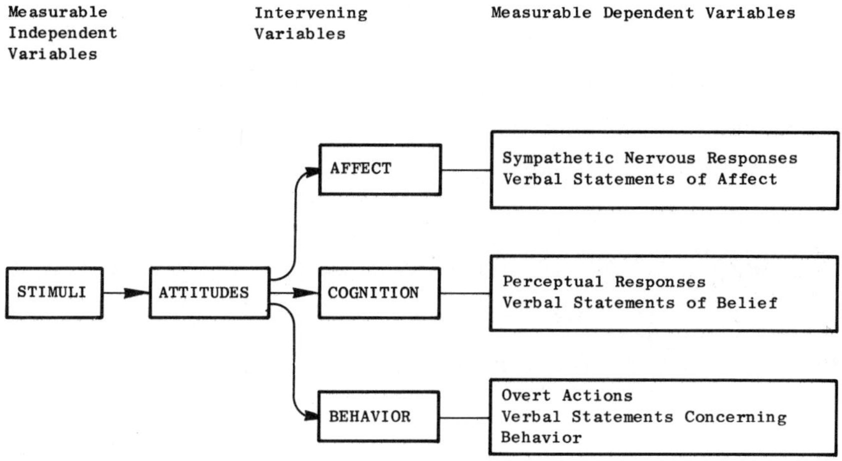

Measurable
Independent
Variables

Intervening
Variables

Measurable Dependent Variables

```
                                  ┌──────────┐   ┌────────────────────────────────────┐
                               ┌─▶│  AFFECT  │───│ Sympathetic Nervous Responses      │
                               │  └──────────┘   │ Verbal Statements of Affect        │
                               │                 └────────────────────────────────────┘
┌─────────┐    ┌───────────┐   │  ┌───────────┐  ┌────────────────────────────────────┐
│ STIMULI │───▶│ ATTITUDES │──▶───│ COGNITION │──│ Perceptual Responses               │
└─────────┘    └───────────┘   │  └───────────┘  │ Verbal Statements of Belief        │
                               │                 └────────────────────────────────────┘
                               │  ┌───────────┐  ┌────────────────────────────────────┐
                               └─▶│ BEHAVIOR  │──│ Overt Actions                      │
                                  └───────────┘  │ Verbal Statements Concerning       │
                                                 │ Behavior                           │
                                                 └────────────────────────────────────┘
```

Figure 1.   The Rosenberg and Hovland (1960) three—component model
of attitudes.

11

responses to questionnaires.

This classification is similar enough to the Rosenberg and Hovland (1960) 'three-component' view of attitudes (see Figure 1) for some comment to be made. Rosenberg and Hovland also distinguished classes of attitude-relevant 'measurable dependent variables', and these they termed the affective, cognitive and behavioral components. 'Verbal statements' were represented within all three components.

In terms of the present schema, I would regard most research on so-called attitude-behavior relations as attempts to predict goal-directed action from linguistic behavior (and perhaps occasionally from emotional reactions, though these might sometimes be included on the behavior side of the equation). Within the Rosenberg and Hovland scheme, such research would be characterized as examining the relations between the different 'components', any of which could be measured through linguistic responses (e.g. Kothandapani, 1971; Ostrom, 1969). Recently, the three-component view has been examined in a particularly useful way by Breckler (1983, 1984). Breckler (1983) first reanalysed the Ostrom (1969) and Kothandapani (1971) using the LISREL computer program in order to establish whether the pattern of intercorrelations between different affective, cognitive and behavioral items suggested that the distinction between the three components was statistically reliable. In neither study was unqualified support found for the three-component model when the data are reanalysed in this way.

Breckler (1984) then went on to propose a number of criteria required for appropriate tests of the three-component view. Among the most pertinent here are that (a) both verbal and non-verbal measures of affect and behavior should be used; and (b) dependent measures of affect, cognition and behavior should take the form of responses to a physically present attitude object. This latter criterion is included because, according to Breckler, if people have to report their affective and behavioral reactions only in the abstract, it is possible that all their reactions might be mainly mediated by the cognitive system. This would result in spurious inflation of the intercorrelations between the three components.

Breckler (1984) reports two studies of his own involving measures of attitudes toward snakes. In the first study, student subjects provided measures of affect, cognition and behavior in the presence of a live snake. Although verbal measures only were used for the cognitive component, indices of affect included measures of heart rate, and subjects' actual approach behaviors (as well as their stated intentions) were recorded. This study showed that the three-component model provided a very good statistical fit to the data. The intercorrelations between the three components were moderate (0.38 for affect/cognition, 0.50 for affect/behavior and 0.70 for cognition/behavior).

In his second study, no live snake was presented and only verbal measures were used for all three components. Although the fit of the model was still relatively good, the three components were less easily distinguished, and the intercorrelations between them were 0.81 or above. These findings therefore emphasize the danger of assuming that different dependent variables necessarily reflect distinct psychological processes, particularly when all involve verbal behavior of one form or other.

Despite these reservations, however, a positive feature of the Rosenberg and Hovland model (for which I gave insufficient credit in my (1980, pp 46-49) discussion) is its resemblance to

13

classifications used in other branches of psychology — notably learning theory, where distinctions may be made between conditioned or unconditioned emotions (affect), expectancies (cognition) and operant responses (behavior). My main misgiving that remains is with their decision not to assign a special status to linguistic behavior, whether it is being used to express belief (to which it is peculiarly suited), affect, or intention.

The main issue, though, is not taxonomy, but the conception of underlying processes. The starting-point of my argument is a simple one, and indeed one that Rosenberg and Hovland would easily have accepted: <u>that attitude-relevant behaviors are acquired through learning</u>. What next needs to be considered, then, is how principles of learning may account for such acquisition. In taking this route, though, we immediately encounter a paradox — we think of 'principles of learning' as making only reluctant distinctions between human beings and other animals, but of attitudes as something distinctively human. Why we do so, I hope, will emerge as the argument proceeds.

It is instructive to compare the Rosenberg and Hovland model with the approach proposed by Greenwald (1968). As may be seen in Figure 2, this too incorporates a distinction between three components (habits, cognitions and emotion). Although the diagram does not explicitly differentiate linguistic from non-linguistic responses, Greenwald uses the distinction between 'cognition' and 'habit' to refer to the distinction "between verbal and nonverbal instrumental response tendencies regarding the attitude object Greenwald, 1968, (p.383)". What is special about Greenwald's proposal is that it attempts to account for the acquisition of different attitude components through the principles of learning accepted at that time. As I shall soon

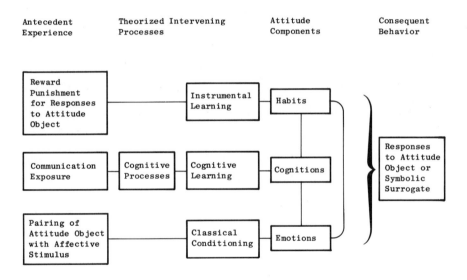

Figure 2. Greenwald's (1968) model of attitudes and learning.

argue, more recent research on learning would tend to go against the implication that the acquisition of habits and emotions depends on qualitatively different forms of learning (instrumental and classical conditioning). Similarly, the distinction between conditioning and 'cognitive learning' may now be less important or easy to draw. These distinctions, however, were only introduced in a quite tentative way:

> "The learning process has been subdivided under the labels 'instrumental learning', 'cognitive learning' and 'classical conditioning' solely as a means of indicating that one may conceive habit-, cognition-, and emotion-acquisition as theoretically separable processes. Similarly, the labeling of specific categories of antecedent experiences is only intended to be suggestive; it is not meant to imply, for example, that cognitions are acquired only from exposure to symbolic communications or that symbolic communications cannot be involved in emotion-acquisition (Greenwald, 1968, pp.364-365)".

The crucial implication here, is that, since habits, cognitions and emotions can be acquired separately, they need not necessarily be consistent withe each other. In other words, whether or not habits, cognitions and emotions go together may well depend on the extent to which they have been acquired together.

Greenwald's emphasis on cognitive learning and on the importance of cognitive responses to persuasion was both innovative and seminal. However, much of the point of talking about 'cognitive' learning was to distinguish theories that gave cognitive processes pride of place from more behavioristic 'S-R' learning theories, the applicability of which Greenwald is prepared to

16

question:

".... S-R discussions of cognitive processes .... currently appear not to rival analyses formulated outside the S-R framework as devices for understanding and predicting cognitive attitude phenomena. It will require much further development before the cognition component of attitude can be analyzed as fully in S-R terms as have been the emotion and habit components.

The potential of learning—behavior theory for analysis of attitudinal cognition is perhaps more apparent in the success of learning—behavior theory formulations that have avoided the restraints of S-R language Greenwald, 1968, (p.384)".

IV. Learning theory and the acquisition of attitudinal responses

Greenwald foreshadows here the pressure that was to build up on learning theorists generally, and not just on those concerned with applications of learning theory to the field of attitudes, for the adoption of less narrowly behavioristic conceptual language. In fact, much recent research on animal learning uses conceptual language that can be surprisingly familiar, even congenial, to social psychologists. In a word, such conceptual language is frequently cognitive, notwithstanding the fact that one is talking mainly about rats, pigeons and such like. Following a tradition that may be traced back to Tolman, learning may be viewed as the acquisition of expectancies (e.g. Tarpy, 1982).

One advantage of the expectancy notion is that it enables stimulus learning (Pavlovian conditioning) and response learning (instrumental conditioning) to be explained in terms of common principles. These principles assume that the function learning serves is to enable animals to predict important events in their environment. Such predictions can be made either on the basis of stimulus events or response events (how the animal has behaved). In addition to changes in measurable response, such expectancies may be associated with different affective or emotional states (e.g. fear).

A crucial assumption of this 'cognitive' approach to animal learning is the idea that conditioned stimuli and responses acquire <u>information value,</u> so that the strength of conditioning depends not simply on the number of previous associations or reinforcements, but on whether a given outcome can be predicted better following a given stimulus (or response) than if this stimulus (or response) has not occurred (Rescorla, 1968). Phenomena such as 'blocking' (Kamin, 1969) are interpreted as showing that once an animal can adequately predict a particular outcome, it does not look for extra information and so may fail to learn about further contingencies associated with that outcome that, from its point of view, would be redundant. There are thus indications of selective processing, cognitive 'miserliness', and possibly even the use of heuristics (cf. Nisbett and Ross, 1980) in animal cognition that have demonstrable effects on behavior.

The essential unity of processes of stimulus and response learning is further shown by studies of 'stimulus-response interactions' where emotional reactions to stimuli produced by Pavlovian conditioning can influence instrumental responding to other stimuli — e.g. superimposing a fear stimulus on an avoidance reaction will increase the intensity of avoidance (Martin and Riess, 1969; Rescorla and Solomon, 1967). Tarpy (1982) argues strongly for an interpretation of such results in terms of interacting conditioned emotional states. This testifies to the close interrelationships between behavioral, cognitive, and affective systems in animals — a message that is interesting not simply in terms of Rosenberg and Hovland's (1960) classification of attitudes into three analogous components, but also in relation to more recent work on the influence of affect and emotion on social cognition (Clark and Fiske, 1982), and of the priming effects of mood and affectively loaded stimuli on memory and judgment (Bower, 1984; Fazio, Powell & Herr, 1983; Higgins, Rholes & Jones, 1977).

The point of all this is that, whereas we tend to think of attitudes as something distinctively human, the 'measurable variables' we take as indicative (or 'expressive') of attitudes may be acquired through processes that we seem to share, to a large extent, with other animals. To a large extent, but not entirely: I am not attempting a reductionist conception of attitudes, but rather adopting the strategy of seeing how far one can go through the application of more general principles.

What the animal literature appears to tell us is that expectancies, emotional states, and adaptive or goal-oriented behaviors tend to be acquired in a closely interrelated manner, but also in relation to very specific stimulus contexts. Put differently, the same stimulus conditions can give rise together to affective, cognitive and behavioral responses. In more human terms, consistency between affect, evaluative beliefs, and behavior is likely to be high so long as one is dealing with responses to the same specific attitude object that have been acquired under the same stimulus conditions. This is exactly the point that Fishbein and Ajzen (1975) make from the standpoint of their model when they demand precise matching of levels of specificity and content among 'attitudinal' and 'behavioral' measures. One the other hand, when affective, cognitive and behavioral responses have been acquired under different stimulus conditions, a lack of correspondence or, in social psychological terms, an apparent attitude-behavior discrepancy may be typical. One

20

would, of course, expect similar stimulus conditions to elicit similar patterns of response through processes of generalization. However, similarity may not always be easy to quantify outside the laboratory independently of the dependent variables it is presumed to influence.

How can this point of view be reconciled with Breckler's (1984) finding of closer correspondence between affective, cognitive and behavioral measures in the _absence_ of the stimulus object? The answer would seem to be that Breckler is not as directly concerned as I am here with hypotheses concerning the processes of _acquisition_ of such responses. Nonetheless, implied in his argument seems to be the suggestion that many cognitive responses may well have been acquired in the abstract, that is in the absence of the actual stimulus object. For this reason, when, as in his second experiment, one obtains verbal (and he suggests hence, cognitively mediated) measures of affect, cognition and behavior in the absence of the stimulus object (a snake) one may well be eliciting responses that have all been acquired in the abstract, or put another way, that all share a common learning history. The high interrelationships between components that he found, therefore, are actually consistent with my present argument.

By the same token, people whose experience of snakes is limited to the printed page, or who have only observed live snakes from the safe side of a sheet of strong plate glass, may well have acquired many things that they can _say_ about snakes (e.g. that they are often not poisonous, that they have beautiful markings on their skin). However, such learnt reactions, evaluative though they are, may not be especially predictive of how these same people would react when provided with a live snake to handle, and this is just what Breckler found. In short, the matter of the physical presence or absence of the stimulus object when attitudinal responses are elicited is quite independent of whether or not these various responses have been acquired under similar or different stimulus conditions. Indeed, the physical presence of the stimulus at the elicitation stage may actually highlight the fact that different response modes have different learning histories.

So we can expect consistency between what Rosenberg and Hovland (1960) would have called the three components of attitude to the extent that the different responses measured are responses that have been acquired under the same stimulus condi- tions — not because of any process of balance, dissonance reduction or whatever, but because such responses share a common learning history. We can, however, expect apparent inconsistency as soon as the stimulus conditions differ, and they may not have to differ by very much. In a similar vein, Fazio (1986) has argued that the accessibility of an attitude from memory — the extent to which it will be "spontaneously" or "automatically" activated by "mere observation" of an attitude object — and the likely degree of attitude—behavior consistency depends on the extent to which the attitude involves "strong object—evaluation associations".

We need to be careful, however, over what might be meant by consistency in the context of animal studies. Here we are talking primarily of events such as animals approaching stimuli associated with food (or some other attractive unconditioned stimuli) and avoiding stimuli associated with aversive states. In the human context, we can scale behaviors on a single evalua- tive dimension analogous to approach—avoidance (indeed many measurement techniques do essentially this) but we are clearly losing information through such a simplification — information that may be vital to any assessment of consistency.

The real difficulty in the human context, though, is not with relating changes in adaptive or goal-directed action to changes in expectancy or emotional state, but with relating any of these to linguistic behavior. Whilst the Rosenberg and Hovland (1960) three-component model provides a quite useful taxonomy of non-linguistic attitudinal responses, it disguises what may be a crucial distinction by dispersing linguistic behavior across the three components according to its content.

Animals do not talk, and we do not tend to talk of animals as having attitudes. The case for assuming language to be vital to attitudes is therefore appealing, but the grounds for accepting it need to be carefully examined. After all, not so long ago, it would have been highly unorthodox for psychologists to talk of rats and pigeons having expectancies, hopes, fears and disappointments. It is not completely inconceivable that future researchers may talk of them having attitudes too. Also, whilst animals do not talk, they clearly do make sounds and use other arbitrary but species-specific signals that can influence the behavior and no doubt emotional states of other conspecifics. Yet we tend to be reluctant to place human linguistic behavior on the same basis as an alarm call. Is such reluctance reasonable?

Such reluctance seems to be based on two sets of assumptions. The first is that we typically assume human utterances to be _intentional_ attempts to communicate meaning (hence the link between the notions of meaning and intention referred to earlier), whereas we do not need to make any such assumption about instinctive alarm calls and other conditioned or unconditioned signaling behavior.   The second is that human linguistic behavior   seems to depend on the acquisition and creative use of rules, such as those of generative grammar, the learning of which, if we believe Chomsky (1959), cannot be explained by Skinnerian principles of operant conditioning (nor, for that matter, by imitation learning — a relatively neglected topic in the animal literature).

The argument in simple terms is that language consists not of a limited set of allowable utterances (that might conceivably be acquired one at a time through imitation and/or instrumental learning) but of a potentially unlimited set of allowable utterances generated by a restricted set of conventional rules that need somehow to be inferred by a speaker—listener from others' linguistic behavior.   What this seems to imply is that, whereas processes of conditioning and imitation may help to shape linguistic behavior, they cannot account completely for how people acquire knowledge of linguistic rules.

The issue here, though, is not with how we acquire know— ledge of linguistic rules, but with how we use them.   Why do we make certain kinds of (linguistically permissible) statements rather than others? It is at least conceivable that the tendency to make particular kinds of statements may sometimes be a function of conditioning and imitation, even though language acquisition as such may not be fully explicable by such principles.   One could argue, indeed, that the kinds of state— ments people make apparently to express their personal feelings and beliefs about particular issues often do not show the kind of boundless creativity which Chomsky and others argue that the rules of language permit.   On the contrary, many attitude state— ments appear to be drawn from a rather limited and familiar repertoire, and, while leaving some room for stylistic embellishment, may be somewhat stereotypic in form and content. The rules of language, however acquired, do not help us to decide whether someone is merely mouthing a slogan, or making a thoughtful personal declaration.

There is thus a real possibility that many of the attitude statements people make could be regarded as conditioned and/or imitative responses – of a rather special kind, certainly, but responses nonetheless. What would be the implications of viewing such linguistic behavior in this way? First, since I am assuming that such linguistic behavior is acquired socially from other people, much of it is likely to be shown in similar forms by large numbers of people. How large will depend on the channels through which people become aware of one another's ways of talking about particular issues, but when we include the mass media within the category of communication channels, we could be dealing with very large numbers indeed. To the extent that attitude statements are socially conditioned/imitative responses, therefore, they are likely to give the impression of widely shared social attitudes.

Are other kinds of attitude-relevant behaviors also likely to be widely shared? Undoubtedly people can imitate non-linguistic forms of behavior, but imitation requires observation and, despite the opportunities provided by television, this may be more difficult on a mass scale than in the case of linguistic behavior. The possibility of attitude-relevant behaviors being widely shared seems directly related to the ease with which they can be recorded and reported. Since linguistic behavior has a special advantage in this respect, we can expect more apparent evidence of widely shared social attitudes in what people say than in other things they do.

What, though, can we expect about the power of such widely shared attitude statements to predict other attitude-relevant behaviors? There is a problem to start with in that widely shared attributes of any kind are not likely to be very discriminative predictors of individual behavioral differences. The more basic issue, though, relates to what we may mean by consistency in the context of responses acquired under non-identical conditions.

V. The relativity of consistency

Consistency is a familiar theme in social psychology, particularly in the theories of attitude organization developed in the 'fifties and 'sixties, (Abelson et al., 1968). These theories are all careful to point out that consistency is not a matter of formal logic, but of perceived implications between different elements. Osgood and Tannenbaum (1955, p.43) for instance, express the central tenet of their congruity theory in the following terms: "Changes in evaluation are always in the direction of increased congruity with the existing frame of reference".

What then becomes important is what defines "the existing frame of reference". In the context of research on judgment, what the phrase suggests is the dimension or dimensions of evaluation selected as the basis for discrimination between objects of judgment. In the outside world, as opposed to the psychophysical laboratory, objects of judgment typically vary simultaneously on a number of separate dimensions. Operationally, it may be useful to distinguish the 'focal' dimension in terms of which discriminations are required, from the 'peripheral' dimensions to which subjects are not required to attend (Eiser and Stroebe, 1972). Variation along such peripheral dimensions, however, can influence judgments along the focal dimension where these different dimensions are correlated with one another (Tajfel, 1959), suggesting a tendency for people to try to reduce subjectively the dimensionality or complexity of objects of judgment with which they are confronted. There are reasons to suppose that this tendency towards reduced dimensionality reflects essentially the same process as the tendency to achieve balance or cognitive consistency (Eiser, 1986, pp 16-17). As pointed out by Jaspars (1965), balanced but not unbalanced trials as defined by Heider (1946), can be represented graphically in terms of what Coombs (1964) would call a unidimensional 'preference space'.

Consistency, then, is not something given by the external world, but something constructed out of it by selective attention to certain attributes or dimensions. Furthermore, many different consistent constructions can be put upon the same situation depending on which dimensions are selected. This, I have argued, may be part of the reason why there are attitudinal disagreements, and why people who take different sides on an issue often seem unable to understand how their opponents can fail to see things the way they do (Eiser, 1975). Measured differences in attitude, that is in overall evaluation, tend to go together with differences in the aspects of an issue people see as salient (van der Pligt and Eiser, 1984). Fazio (1986) proposes that this process of selective perception is crucial to any relationship between attitudes and behavior, since the "influence of attitudes upon behavior occurs as a result of the impact that attitudes have upon perceptions of the attitude object in the immediate situation and upon definitions of the event... without such selective perception attitudes would not affect behavior (p.230)".

If consistency, whether among attitudes and cognitions or between attitudes and behavior, depends on the selection of salient attributes to define the frame of reference, what influences salience? There is likely to be more than one answer to this question. One factor will be the accessibility of affects and cognitions from memory (Fazio et al., 1983; Higgins et al., 1977). In the contexts of attributions and cognitive schemata, Taylor and others have argued in a similar way for stimulus distinctiveness as an important determinant of salience (Taylor and Fiske, 1978; Taylor, Fiske, Etcoff and Ruderman 1978). The same notion could be phrased in terms of figure—ground relation-ships, or in terms of new learning being prompted by unexpected stimulus events. Also of relevance is the tendency not to attend to stimulus attributes that seem redundant for purposes of pre-diction (Kamin, 1969; Rescorla, 1971).

The concept of 'attribute' in the context of attitudi-nal judgment is not without its difficulties. Often what one is talking about is a dimension of description rather than an easily distinguishable physical attribute (such as skin color or gen-der, as in the Taylor et al., 1978 research). In other words, one is observing differences in people's use of <u>judgmental language</u> or category labels. To regard such effects as dependent on language and labeling is not to downgrade their importance. On the contrary, the manner in which an event is labeled can determine how it is subsequently processed. For instance, once an event has been encoded in the terms of a linguistic category label, it is the category label that seems to be stored in memory rather than the details of the event itself (Higgins & Lurie, 1983).

THE EXPRESSION OF ATTITUDE

In a typical social judgment experiment, the judgmental language available to subjects is determined by the experimenter. However, the way in which subjects will _use_ a particular scale to communicate differentiations between the stimuli presented to them depends on their own evaluations of the stimuli, on the stimulus context, and on both the connotative and denotative meaning of the terms used to label the different ends or regions of the scale. In general, our findings suggest that people will make more extreme or polarized discriminations among stimuli in terms of language that is more appropriate for the range of stimulus values presented (Eiser and van der Pligt, 1982), and more consistent in terms of implied connotations with their own subjective classifications of the stimuli (Eiser and Mower White, 1974, 1975).

A particularly well—replicated finding is that people will make more polarized discriminations along response scales that are labeled so as to be evaluatively consistent with their own acceptance—rejection of the objects of judgment (typically, atti—tude statements), so that people will prefer to use judgmental language that allows them to describe their own viewpoints in terms that imply a positive evaluation (Eiser and van der Pligt, 1984; van der Pligt and van Dijk, 1979). There is some evidence too, that people may shift their expressed agreement/disagreement with attitude statements so as to achieve greater consistency with the evaluative implications of the language they are using (Eiser and Pancer, 1979; Eiser and Ross, 1977).

People with different attitudes thus will define their frame of reference in terms of different sets of values. Opponents of unilateral nuclear disarmament, for example, may seek to justify their position in terms of 'the need for national security', whereas proponents may use phrases such as 'the future of life on our planet'. What is interesting theoretically is that attitudinal differences do not seem to rest primarily (although they may partly do so) on disagreements over whether such values are 'good' or 'bad', but on disagreements over whether they are at issue, and how. Thus an opponent of unilateral nuclear disarmament might seek to play down the extent of destruction that would be caused by a nuclear war, and argue that it is the 'balance of fear' that has prevented nuclear weapons being used. On the other hand, a supporter of disarmament might deny that retaining nuclear weapons increases our national security, arguing instead that it makes us a more likely target for nuclear attack.

Is national security an 'attribute' of the issue of nuclear disarmament? It certainly is not in the sense that, for instance, skin or hair color are 'attributes' of people's physical appearance. It may however be a _value_ which some people see as relevant and which they adopt as a criterion for the acceptance or rejection of specific points of view. Other people, though, may use other criteria, that is define their own frame of reference in terms of other values.

Consistency (in the sense the term is used in 'consistency' theories of attitudes) depends upon evaluative frames of reference that are more general˘ than the specific objects of judgment being evaluated. The function of such frames of reference is to enable a person to think of different concepts in relation to one another — concepts which otherwise might be regarded as _un_related. This is at a different level from the kind of consistency we may observe within people's (or animals') expectancies and emotional responses to _specific_ stimuli, where

31

we are dealing with contiguous reactions elicited under the same environmental conditions.

If we assume that consistency is relative to the existing frame of reference, what can we make of the hypothesis that people are motivated to resolve inconsistency? Where does such motivation come from? My impression is that most consistency theorists would offer an answer in terms of intrapsychic factors, such as homeostasis, Praegnanz etc. Festinger (1957), for example, conceived of dissonance as a state of noxious arousal. Such approaches all seem to assume something 'natural' about consistency and aberrant about inconsistency. There are exceptions to this view. Bem (1967) seeks to explain dissonance 'effects' in terms of self-attribution processes rather than the reduction of any intrapsychic arousal. More recently, Cooper and Fazio (1984), whilst arguing for the importance of arousal in the dissonance process, have proposed that "dissonance has precious little to do with inconsistency among cognitions per se (p.234)" and that what produces noxious arousal is the feeling that one may have been responsible for foreseeable but unwanted consequences. Furthermore, "Like the arousal involved in emotions, the state of dissonance requires appropriate interpretation and labeling for attitude change to occur (p.244)".

Various researchers in the tradition of balance theory, have stressed the importance of biases other than 'Heiderian' consistency (e.g. Gollob, 1974). Streufert and Streufert (1978) have described the appeal and adaptiveness of cognitive complexity as well as cognitive simplicity. However, an even more challenging possibility may need to be faced — that consistency is not a natural state of affairs but rather a condition attained only precariously, with difficulty, and in response to the demands of

<u>others</u>.

Let me review the argument so far as it relates to questions of consistency and attitude-behavior discrepancy.

1) Many apparently attitude-relevant responses may be regarded as conditioned responses. Where such responses share a common learning history, and hence are under the control of the same stimuli, there is every reason to expect consistency between affect (emotional responses), cognition (expectancies) and behavior (instrumental or goal-directed actions). There is no reason, however, to attribute such consistency to any special motivational principle, still less to any moral sense or "self-regarding sentiment" (McDougall, 1908). Principles of stimulus-response interaction would allow us to predict the same effects for pigeons or rats.

2) Verbal statements of attitude, too, may be considered (possibly) as conditioned or imitative responses. However, they constitute a separate special category in that it is by no means certain that they share the same learning history as the more immediate responses considered in the preceding paragraph. Furthermore, the stimuli which elicit such verbal responses will not necessarily be the attitude objects to which such statements refer. (Verbal expressions of racial prejudice and stereotyping, for instance, may be made by people who have never met a member of the stereotyped group). If one wants to identify the stimuli controlling such responses one needs to specify the conditions under which such statements are made, and a not insignificant feature of such conditions is almost certainly going to be <u>the presence of others</u>. So — since verbal statements of attitude do not share the same learning history as the other categories of attitude-relevant responses here considered, one would <u>not</u> neces-

sarily expect verbal and non-verbal responses to be 'consistent' with each other.

3) The term 'consistency' may also be used to refer to stability over time. Such stability may be predicted in accordance with conditioning principles, so long as the stimulus conditions show no marked change. This could apply to both verbal and non-verbal responses. However the same attitude objects may well elicit different (e.g. affective) reactions depending on the conditions under which they are perceived.

The above three stages to the argument essentially summarize the extent to which we might expect different kinds of consistency and discrepancy on the basis of simple learning principles. There is nothing particularly human about any of this. Now, though, some extra principle needs to be introduced:

4) 'Consistency' in the sense the term is used in theories of attitude organization, is relative to a selective frame of reference. This frame of reference is often defined on the basis of value-laden criteria, and may be reflected in people's use of judgmental language.

VI. The learning of accountability

Social behavior involves being able to predict the responses of others to one's own behavior. This need not demand any especially sophisticated cognitive activity, so long as other's responses are treated as just another stimulus event. What does require a higher level of sophistication — a level I feel no temptation to assume is attained by rats or pigeons — is to be able to predict others' expectations concerning one's own behavior. Seeing others as thinking beings, to whom one is oneself an object (but also an active object of perception) seems .to involve a qualitative leap in complexity of cognitive functioning — to what Langford (1978) has termed "reciprocal self-awareness."

Coming to see oneself as others see one has been a familiar theme in many psychological theories from that of William James (1910) onwards. My concern here is with something slightly narrower — the question of how we learn about others' expectations concerning our own behavior. I am assuming for the sake of argument that such learning is not necessarily different in principle from other kinds of learning, at least to the extent that it involves acquisition of expectancies concerning 'if-then' contingencies. I am also assuming that we are in some sense motivated to conform to the expectations that others hold of us. The form that such motivation takes is not too critical for the present argument. It will of course vary in strength and depend on which particular other people we are talking about. All that matters here is that those aspects of others' behavior toward us that reflect their expectations about our own behavior constitute important events that we seek to try to predict. They are, in other words, events with reinforcement value.

There has, of course, been a considerable amount of research of indirect relevance to this issue concerned with processes of self—presentation and impression management (e.g. Baumeister, 1982; Tetlock and Manstead, 1985). Most of this work has been guided by the assumption that individuals want to present socially desirable images of themselves. This has led to ques— tions about whether or not individual's genuinely believe that they have the positive characteristics that they are presenting. One example of this has been in terms of the application of impression management notions to the interpretation of attitude change in studies of cognitive dissonance. At first, this approach involved the assumption that the apparent change produced in these studies was not genuine, and that subjects were deliberately responding in a way that was discrepant from their private opinions (Tedeschi, Schlenker & Bonoma, 1971), but this assumption seems no longer to be insisted upon. More recently Tedeschi and Rosenfeld (1981) and Schlenker (1982) have talked in terms of feelings such as social anxiety, embarrassment, and the need to protect a positive view of one's own identity, that give rise to a motivation to act in such a way as to obtain and retain others' approval.

This general principle that we try to conform to others'

expectations does not lead necessarily to any prediction of greater consistency in attitudes or behavior — not, that is, unless we assume that other people selectively reinforce through their social approval or whatever certain kinds of consistency. If others formed expectations of how we should behave as though they were unbiased observers, there is no reason to suppose that they would expect us to be more consistent than we would be anyway if left to our own devices. However, other people are not neutral about our behavior — they have a stake in our consistency. This is because we are also part of their world which they are trying to predict, <u>and if we can be made more consistent, we will thereby be more predictable</u>. Both society at large and more immediate personal relationships demand that our behavior achieves a reasonable level of apparent consistency — less than total consistency for sure, but still much more than that likely to be produced merely by different responses having a common learning history.

It should, however, be stressed that particular kinds of inconsistency may be socially sanctioned and indeed demanded in certain circumstances. <u>Complete</u> consistency or observation of rules may be synonymous with inflexibility and rigidity, and the norm of consistency may often therefore be counterbalanced by the norm of preparedness to 'consider individual cases on their merits', to 'make exceptions' and generally to be ready to maintain some distance from a prescribed role or the rules associated with a particular social position, category or relationship (cf. Billig, 1985; also Eiser, 1986, pp. 287–292).

How might certain kinds of consistency be selectively reinforced? A young boy comes home from school and announces that "Tom isn't my friend 'ny more" (Tom being his favorite companion of the last four months), yet the next day asks if Tom can come and play and seems surprised when his parents raise doubts about whether it's a good idea. What is happening here is some mis-match between the boy's behavior and his parents' expectations. Or imagine a young girl who invites her friends to "a party on Saturday", without checking the arrangements with her parents. Come Saturday she forgets about the 'arrangement' until three of her friends arrive on the doorstep with their parents: again a mismatch of child behavior with adult expectations. How might these mismatches be interpreted? The temptation is to assume that the boy didn't 'really mean' he disliked Tom, and that the girl didn't 'really mean' she wanted a party — but we must be careful not to make adult assumption about what "really mean" really means.

In both examples, two kinds of extra consistency seem to be demanded by the adults over and above that shown by the child. The first extra kind of consistency involves the assumption of stability of likes and wants over time. So the boy might be told "You can't just stop and start friendships when you feel like it", and the girl might be told "You can't just want a party one minute and then decide you don't." But in riposte to each of these, one could ask a resounding "Why not?", to which the only real answer would have to be "Because adult society doesn't work that way". Heider (1958) and subsequent researchers refer to a bias in social cognition termed the "fundamental attribution error". This involves a tendency to attribute behavior to stable dispositions of the actor rather than unstable aspects of the situation. The argument is that we may be 'biased' towards expecting more cross-situational consistency in behavior (or for that matter feelings and thoughts) than is 'really' there (Ross,

38

1977). But is this 'bias' just an error, or a search for predic- tability that in some instances may be self-fulfilling. A large part of becoming socialized may involve acquiring enough cross- situational stability in what we want and like and feel and do to be recognizable and predictable to other people with whom we interact.

And in what way we say: this is the other kind of consis- tency that is critically involved. Words are not just sounds, but can be taken (at least by adults) to imply social obligations over time. Saying that Tom is or isn't a "friend" is not to be taken just as a token of one's affection (or lack of it) right at the moment, but as something that is to be taken as a guide for organizing future relationships and interactions. To "invite" friends to a party is not just an expression of a "Wouldn't it be nice?" but feeling a commitment actually to have a party unless it is canceled. The meaning of consistency in these contexts depends absolutely on the social construction put upon the con- cepts of 'friendship' and 'invitation' in our society. There is nothing absolute about such concepts. Other societies may not hold their members accountable in quite the same ways. Nonethe- less, such assumptions of accountability are part of the way these concepts — and words — are used. Again, a large part of becoming socialized may involve acquiring an understanding of culturally defined norms of accountability — learning that we can be held accountable in what we do for what we say, and vice versa. In order to learn what words mean we need to learn what words do. This is especially so for the words we use to describe our feelings.

Learning such rules of social accountability may be quite difficult. The feedback from others' reactions may often be

39

ambiguous, so we may have reason to doubt that others understand the relevant words and concepts in the way we have tried to use them. The rules themselves may change and vary within and between families, social classes, regions and so on. What this suggests is an asynchrony between one's acquisition on the one hand of a repertoire of verbal statements apparently expressive of feelings, thoughts, intentions and so on, and on the other hand, of an understanding of the <u>social</u> rules that define the appropriate contexts in which such statements may be used. In other words, people may learn a variety of verbal expressions well before, and sometimes no doubt without ever, fully learning the social constructions others will put upon such statements.

The question "How do we know that people really mean what they say?" seems basic to whether we are going to be prepared to take verbal statements as indicators of someone's attitude. Unfortunately, it is a question that can never be answered on the basis of information from any single speech act considered in isolation. We cannot translate it into a question of whether the speech act was 'deliberate'. The issue is not one of intentionality, but of the use of social knowledge. A speaker may say something quite deliberately without anticipating quite how it will be interpreted by others. For both listeners and speakers there is a problem of assessing the appropriateness of both one's own, and others', use of language.

Many verbal statements of attitude, therefore, will tend to be 'irresponsible' in the non-pejorative sense that they have been made without an adequate appreciation of the expectations they will create for the listener. The acquisition through socialization of rules of social accountability serves to reduce such 'irresponsibility', but is unlikely to eliminate it entirely. Some discrepancy between verbal and other indicators of attitude is thus only to be expected.

VII. Values, salience and accountability

But now we run into a new complication: <u>there are different ways in which we can be held accountable</u>. As long as we confine our attention to people's understanding of relatively simple statements and behavioral sequences, one can describe the implied social knowledge in terms of notions such as 'scripts' (Schank and Abelson, 1977) or role-rule context (Harre and Secord, 1972). The kind of consistency demanded many for such statements and sequences to be interpreted as meaningful is relatively straightforward (e.g. children should want to play with their friends, waitresses in restaurants should bring us food). However, as I have pointed out, the consistency in someone's political beliefs, for instance, is relative to the frame of reference in terms of which we choose to evaluate them — <u>and we have a choice</u>.

To say that there are alternative evaluative frames of reference in terms of which the consistency of our attitudes may be assessed amounts to saying that there are alternative values with respect to which we may be held accountable, and seek (or have) to justify what we say and do. Salient dimensions in the context of judgment may be thought of as implying salient arguments that can be used to justify our preferences or actions. Just as people with opposing viewpoints can each see their own positions as internally consistent and their opponents' as inconsistent, so they can each produce arguments that constitute efficient accounts or justifications for their own point of view.

Do individuals differ in the values they acquire? Of course, but attitudinal and behavioral differences are still likely even among people who seem to share the same sets of values. On the one hand, certain values may be held only by certain groups of people. The value of 'doing God's will' would not be a relevant one for an atheist, for instance. On the other hand, there may be some values that appear to be very widely shared indeed — kindness, happiness, peace, personal freedom, the preservation of life, and so on. There may be individual differences in the relative importance people attach to different values of these kinds, so that some people may say they value peace more than happiness, whereas others may order values the other way around. Indeed, this is the main message of Rokeach's (e.g. 1979) research. Nonetheless all these values could potentially be invoked by anyone to justify or persuade. Billig (1985) expresses a very similar idea when he talks of the alternative forms of rhetoric that people will use in different situations, so that even racists may use the rhetoric of racial tolerance in specific contexts. Where people with different attitudes really seem to differ is in the ways they bring such general values to bear on specific issues.

A very common way this can happen is that people may decline to apply a value that they hold in the abstract to a specific point at issue. Take, for example, the issue of abortion. Its opponents see this as an issue of the sanctity of life, its supporters as one of personal freedom (and this is reflected in the names by which action groups can choose to identify themselves). Yet this does not mean that, in other contexts, anti-abortionists will deny that they value personal freedom, or pro-abortionists that they value life. This kind of selectivity of preferred values reflects the same principle I discussed earlier in relation to people's selective preference for different kinds of judgmental language.

A good example of how abstract values may or may not relate to specific attitudes and behavior comes from the study of health-related behavior. One might suppose that people who value health particularly highly will be more likely to engage in a whole range of behaviors aimed at preventing the occurrence of illness or injury. According to Kristiansen (1985), however, matters are not nearly so simple. Kristiansen's subjects ranked the values listed in Rokeach's (1967) Terminal Value Survey, with the additional value health included, and also indicated the extent to which they engaged in each of a list of 15 preventive health behaviors. Kristiansen found that the relative position subjects assigned to health in their hierarchy of values was predictive of the extent to which they sought to protect themselves from risks that were classified as direct, but less so when the risks were indirect. Moreover, a number of other values, especially that of an exciting life made important contributions to behavioral prediction. Kristiansen suggests that health education might make fuller use of techniques of value confrontation that aim to increase people's awareness of apparent contradictions between their values, behavior and aspects of their self-concept.

To such strategies of stressing certain values at the

expense of others and of getting people to think about the behavioral implications of the values that they hold, may be added
that of linking shared values to a specific issue in special or
novel ways. Thus, advocates of the need for a nuclear deterrent
object to the way that supporters of disarmament refer to themselves as the "peace movement". They would argue that they also
value peace highly, and that the disarmers are attempting to
present a shared value as though it were a discriminating one.
The validity or reasonableness of such arguments is not the
theoretical point at issue. What is important is that, for
people who hold such attitudes, their frames of reference are
defined largely by the arguments they use and the language in
terms of which their arguments are expressed. It is in terms of
such arguments and such language that their attitudes and behavior are to be seen as consistent, predictable, and hence as
understandable.

The need to render one's behavior and feelings understandable to others, then, seems to underly people's acquisition
of these broader kinds of attitudinal consistency too. Again,
though, individuals may differ in the manner and in the extent to
which they acquire understanding of the relevant rules of accountability. Some may employ a relatively simple moral code involving the application of a rather limited set of values and
arguments across a whole range of different issues. Others may
acquire a greater versatility to introduce a wide variety of
alternative values and arguments even within the context of a
single topic. Such individual differences may well relate to
theoretical questions concerning cross-situational stability of
personality, cognitive complexity and simplicity, authoritaria-
nism and so on.

Consistency (or inconsistency) of this broader kind is essentially meaningless without the use of abstract concepts that allow different feelings, beliefs and behaviors to be grouped together subjectively in alternative, non-obligatory and often innovative ways. Such grouping does not seem to rely on shared eliciting stimuli controlling the different responses, nor on stimulus or response generalization. (Why should one generalize along just these particular dimensions of comparison rather than any others?). Such concepts, I would assert, cannot be acquired, still less communicated, without the use of language.

The kind of language that needs to be used, however, serves more than just the function of taxonomic description, or even that of evaluation. It serves a persuasive or gerundive function (cf. Nowell-Smith, 1956). It conveys not only what we feel, but what we feel others should feel, and by implication, what they should do. If we say "That's an unkind thing to do", we are not simply reporting negative affect, but saying "That shouldn't be done" or, if we are addressing the actor, "Don't do that". This is all part of the fact that attitudinal judgments are not mere expressions of private feelings, but special kinds of statements about external reality. We want others to share our views of such external reality, agreeing with us about what is good and what ought to be done. The communication of salient values through language, therefore, is a way of communicating normative expectations concerning, not just private feelings, but behavior — expectations that we must also accept as applicable to ourselves.

It is thus not simply our evaluations that may come to be consistent with an "existing frame of reference" but also our behavior. Attitude-behavior consistency, in the sense of consistency between verbal behavior and goal—directed action, thus depends on our being prepared to see our own goal—directed actions as accountable in terms of the same criteria on which we base our verbal expressions of approval or disapproval. Put differently, if the principles by which we make value judgments are the same as those by which we define the goals to which our actions are oriented, we should expect greater attitude—behavior consistency. Viewed in this way, consistency between verbal behavior and goal—directed action is not something that occurs as a matter of course unless other variables (cf. Wicker, 1969) intervene. It is something acquired, if at all, as a result of a difficult process of social learning and in order to accommodate to social demands. It requires (a) that we learn that evaluative language implies generalizable ethical principles (b) that we define the goals of our social actions in terms of such prin—ciples, and (c) that we apply the same principles across situa—tions and to different aspects of our behavior (i.e. that we consider different aspects of our behavior within a common frame of reference).

This last stipulation is absolutely crucial, and its arbitrariness must be recognized. Goal—oriented action that seems 'inconsistent' with verbal behavior is not necessarily 'unprincipled'. An accusation of inconsistency in such a context is no more than a demand that both types of response be guided by a single principle. The reasonableness of such a demand depends on how reasonable it is to rule out of consideration alternative potentially applicable principles. A common feature of the rhetoric employed by those advocating simplistic moral or politi—cal creeds is the attempt to universalize certain principles or values while neglecting other principles or declaring them to be

47

illegitimate.

Such rhetoric requires language, but once we consider language as part of rhetoric (cf. Billig, 1985) we must assign language a more active and potent status than merely that of conditioned verbal responses. Language provides us with the capacity to refer to objects or eventualities that are not physically present, and to discuss ideas in the abstract. It allows us to express negation and hence disagreement, and it enables us to <u>argue</u>. The processes of argumentation, in terms especially of the elaboration of logical, practical and ethical implications are basic to human thought. They are assumed implicitly or explicitly in theories of attitude structure and change — for instance cognitive consistency theory, and more recent research on cognitive responses to persuasion (Petty & Cacioppo, 1985). It may be here, if anywhere, that we should look for distinctive differences between the evaluative experiences of human beings on the one hand and animals without language on the other.

VIII. Attitude and the pyschology of judgment

Traditional attitude research has confused the issue of the consistency of attitude-relevant responses with that of their accuracy as indicators of attitude. My argument here is that these issues are quite distinct. I have proposed that such response consistency can result from separate responses sharing contiguous learning histories and from external pressures for social accountability. Neither kind of consistency entails that we view the responses thereby produced as more or less accurate or 'sincere' reflections of any internal state.

But what kind of internal state? Here, as I have argued, the traditional approach treats attitudes as private, unobservable thoughts and feelings that somehow 'cause' publicly observable responses. The key point, though, is that, for such thoughts and feelings to be experienced as <u>attitudes</u>, they must be experienced as related to subjects or events in the external world. Indeed, the attitudes people report can be influenced by manipulation of the apparent causes of feelings of arousal (Cooper, Zanna and Taves, 1978; Fazio, Zanna and Cooper, 1977). An attitude, then, is not a kind of unlabeled mood, but an experience that involves a particular a way of <u>representing</u> the environment. This representation is _expressed_ in terms of attitude-relevant responses. It will be selective, value-laden and partly self-referring. We ourselves are part of the environment we seek to represent.

The relationship between attitude and behavior may thus be conceptualized in terms of the very simple schema shown in Figure 3. This schema comprises three elements: the environment; a representational system, and a response system. The function of the representational system is to interpret the environment, and to monitor responses. The response system generates responses from the internal representation, these responses are monitored by the representational system and also produce changes in the environment. Both the representational system and the response system will be influenced by learning.

The nature of the representational system has been the predominant concern of social cognition research over recent years. Concepts such as categories, schemata, information-processing and attributions are but a few of those that relate explicitly to our interpretations of our social world. When we consider other branches of psychology, a similar emphasis on the representational is to be discerned — in the fields of perception and cognition obviously, but also, as has been mentioned, in animal learning research. As learning research has become less 'behaviorist' and more 'cognitive' the central issue has become one of identifying the cognitive structures (in this context, 'if-then' expectancies) in terms of which animals interpret their environment.

There is thus a vast amount of very varied but complementary research on the nature of the representational system. There are ways of representing the environment (essentially, any non-

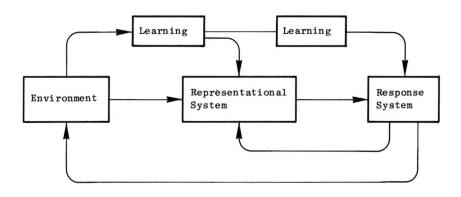

Figure 3. A simple schema of the attitude—behavior relationship.

evaluative way) to which the term 'attitude' would be inappropriate. Beyond that it is unnecessary, for the present argument at least, to be more specific. Indeed, it may be positively misleading to talk of attitudes as though they could be <u>purely</u> defined in terms of categories, schemata, expectancies, or whatever.

This predominance of cognitive theorizing, however, has meant that the response system has received somewhat less attention. Thus the attribution literature, for example, has been more concerned until recently with the antecedents of attributions than with their behavioral consequences (Kelley and Michela, 1980). The issue of how responses are generated by internal representations is considered by animal learning theorists, but the problem appears in a relatively simple form — e.g. one assumes a direct relationship between stimulus valence and approach—avoidance. But even here there are surprises. One area of research is concerned with how animals match the strength of their response to the value of a reward (e.g. pigeons will peck more vigorously at response keys associated with more frequent reinforcements). Attempts to quantify this relationship have come up with a 'matching law' that, as proposed by Herrnstein (1961), is formally identical to that proposed by Anderson (1976) to describe how people make judgments of the degree of inequitableness of inputs and outputs. Within social psychology, a dominant tradition has been expectancy—value theory. Simply stated, this assumes that people will choose to perform behaviors associated with higher expected values or subjective expected utilities. Research on human decision—making has identified numerous exceptions to this principle, albeit often in the context of rather unreal experimental tasks invol—

ving preferences for different kinds of hypothetical risks or gambles. Within social psychology perhaps the most familiar current application of the expectancy—value principle is that embodied in the Fishbein and Ajzen (1975) model of attitudes and behavioral intentions. However, regardless of whether Fishbein and Ajzen are offering an adequate account of attitude formation (cf. van der Pligt and Eiser, 1984), their model makes no pretence at describing the response system as a whole. All it attempts to predict is the formulation of intentions assumed to underlie goal—directed action.

Neither a conditioning approach nor an expectancy—value approach offer a full account of a response system that is in large part _expressive_, that is, where the form of the overt response (e.g. the words used) and its relation to any internal state depends on arbitrary conventions. Indeed, the most difficult aspect of any conditioning approach to attitude forma—tion is probably that of specifying the units or levels of expressive behavior that are susceptible to the effects of rein—forcement (see e.g. Greenwald, 1968). Research in the psychology of judgment however, conceptualizes the response system in a way that is ideally suited to dealing with expressive behavior.

There is a long tradition in judgment research of distingui—shing between the objective physical attributes of stimuli (their 'physical magnitude'), the subjective experience of the same stimuli (their 'psychological magnitude'), and the way in which they are rated along some response continuum or judgment scale. The early psychophysicists were concerned with finding laws to describe the relationship between psychological and physical magnitudes, using ratings of the stimuli as an index of psycholo—

53

gical magnitude. More recent research has examined how changes in stimulus context can lead to changes in the perceived and/or judged values of the stimuli presented, and has also attended to factors that influence how subjective experiences are represented in terms of ratings (e.g. Anderson, 1975; Parducci, 1963; Stevens, 1958).

There are many ways in which such notions are applicable to attitudes (see Eiser, 1984; Eiser and Stroebe, 1972). For instance, Upshaw (1969) distinguishes the 'content' of a person's attitude from its 'rating' and, in subsequent research, demonstrates that some social influence manipulations can have a effect primarily on rating (Upshaw, Ostrom and Ward, 1970; Upshaw, 1978). More recently, Upshaw and Ostrom (1984) go on to stress that there are many alternative dimensions along which a person can express judgments of a stimulus.

> "There are obviously very many ways in which attitudes are expressed: donations of time and money to political or social causes, words of praise and blame, joining picket lines, and so forth. Any of these models of expression might function as a judgmental medium (Upshaw and Ostrom, 1984, p.31).

This argument follows on from the observation made by many judgment researchers that almost any kind of behavior that can be controlled by the subject, so as to produce an ordered continuum of responses, is a potential medium for the expression of one's experience of a stimulus. Rating scales printed on question-naires or linked to computer keyboards are obviously convenient, but one can as easily (if less conveniently) ask subjects to squeeze hand dynamometers, pour beans out of a jar, fill in outline diagrams of a thermometer and so on. Upshaw and Ostrom

(1984) use the concept of 'congeneric scales' to refer to response continua that are alternative ways of describing a given internal state or 'latent variable', and in an important footnote make the following point:

"We find it difficult to distinguish between attitude and behavior as many have done. Given our conception of attitude content as a latent variable, we view the person as seeking ways to express the latent attitude. Any expression is a behavior, and it is also a judgment. In this sense one can learn about attitude content only by inference from behavior (Upshaw & Ostrom, 1984, p.31)".

In terms of the argument of this paper, what this passage means is that any attitude-relevant response, verbal or non-verbal, may be consid-ered as a judgmental medium for the expression of a person's internal representation of an attitude object. In a similar vein, Upmeyer (1981) argues that:

"social judgment should be considered a two-step process. The first step consists of the perception, storage and internal representation of some stimulus or stimuli. The second step consists of a response which may be thought of as the external presentation of an internal representation (Upmeyer, 1981, p.257)".

Using concepts borrowed from signal detection theory, Upmeyer goes on to distinguish factors that influence 'differentiation ability' on the one hand, and 'response tendency, on the other. He takes the term 'differentiation ability' to refer to processes of "stimulus perception and repre-sentation memory" and of the "emergence of a differentiation task and formation of subjective distributions", 'response ten-dency", on the other hand, refers to the "decision as to whether to respond" and the "decision among response alternatives" (p.263). Thus, factors such as selective attention are to be considered as influencing differentiation ability, and others such as social desirability as influencing response tendency.

More recently Roth and Upmeyer (1985) have gone on to consider responses on more than one modality (or as Upshaw and Ostrom would put it, on more than one congeneric scale) — specifically verbal and non-verbal expressions of mirth when cartoons were presented in different contexts. Their data suggest a distinction between factors influencing subjects' mean levels of response on the one hand, and the correlations between their ratings and non-verbal expressions on the other.

In terms of the schema shown in Figure 3, then, we start with attitude objects in the environment that are represented subjectively within the representational system, and then assume that the response system generates, from these representations, expressive behavior along a number of response modalities or 'congeneric scales'. The representational system, it is assumed, can also, in principle, monitor the level of response within any single modality and the degree of 'matching' or consistency of responses across modalities. Attitude-relevant responses are thus distinguished from the internal representations they express. However, these internal representations are <u>representations</u> of stimuli in the environment. In other words, attitude-relevant responses are <u>about</u>, and have as their reference, objects and events in the external environment. What such responses <u>express</u> may be termed a latent variable or a subjective representation but what they are responses <u>to</u> are stimuli in the environment.

IX. Judgment and learning

How may such notions be squared with the suggestion that
some attitude—relevant responses at least may be seen as the
product of conditioning? There is no basic contradiction. Theories of both judgment and learning describe relationships between
environmental stimuli on the one hand and behavior on the other.
Both approaches (now) attempt to understand such relationships
in terms of how the stimuli are subjectively represented. The
approaches seem to diverge to the extent that judgment theorists,
unlike learning theorists, tend to treat the responses they are
interested in as consciously intended, whereas learning theorists
are more likely to concern themselves as much with subjects'
representations of the expected consequences of a response as
with their representations of the stimulus to which that response
occurs.

My view is that such differences are more apparent than
real. The issue of consciousness becomes less important to the
extent that it is thought of in terms of monitoring rather than
control processes (though for some kinds of control, monitoring
may be vital). Response expectancies may also influence
judgments more than is sometimes acknowledged. If one allows, as

57

on the evidence one must, that judgmental or expressive responses are influenced by people's expectations of how they will be interpreted by others, then one must acknowledge the relevance of response expectancies to judgmental behavior.

Relating the two theoretical traditions to each other can help in highlighting important features of both the representational system and the response system. Viewed from the standpoint of learning theory, the prime function of the representational system is that of <u>predicting</u> important environmental events: such prediction depends on the <u>discrimination</u> of stimulus situations and the acquisition of <u>expectancies</u> associated with such situations. A large part of both learning and judgment research may be seen as related to the question of when and why a conceivably detectable stimulus difference does or does not elicit a difference in response. If important events can be predicted on the basis of one kind of stimulus discrimination, the subject is less likely to attend to or learn about other stimulus attributes. This is directly relevant to what Upmeyer (1981) terms 'differentiation ability', and to what I have discussed earlier under the heading of 'salience'.

As for the response system, notions drawn from learning theory can also help us understand some of the factors influencing what Upmeyer (1981) calls 'response tendency.' I have argued that many forms of attitude-relevant behavior should be considered as conditioned responses to stimuli, with separate responses having separate learning histories. But to which stimuli are such responses conditioned? Animal experiments use deliberately artificial situations so that the experimenter has maximum control over the stimuli presented to the subject. No such control is possible in human social interaction. Thus we can never be entirely sure that an attitude-relevant response only reflects the person's representation of the attitude object to which it ostensibly refers. It may be partly under the stimulus control of <u>other</u> features of the situation in which it is elicited.

The presence of other people, whether known or unknown to the individual, may be a powerful stimulus, since many attitude-relevant responses are typically acquired in the presence of others and performed so as to be observable by others. It also may be rare for attitude objects to be experienced in isolation from other stimuli. When a politician is applauded at an election rally, is such applause a reaction to the content of the speech, the style of its delivery, the politician's physical appearance, the excitement of being in a large crowded hall, the presence of television cameras, or whatever? Such questions relate closely to the work of Chaiken (1980) on 'heuristic' versus 'systematic' information-processing in response to persuasion, and to that of Petty and Cacioppo (1985) on 'central' and 'peripheral' routes to persuasion.

From the point of view of judgment, such extraneous stimuli need careful consideration. If all they do is change the mean level of response within a given modality, such a change in response tendency should still leave the correlation between different response modalities unaffected. In other words, a situationally-produced response bias need not detract from the discriminative reliability of a set of responses.

'Biased' responses may still provide reliable information if the 'bias' is simply due to extraneous stimuli magnifying or suppressing the likelihood of a particular response to an attitude object. A greater difficulty would arise if extraneous stimuli were capable of eliciting _apparently_ attitude-relevant responses regardless of the person's internal representation (if any) of the attitude object.

The very real possibility of this occurring, both for verbal and non-verbal behavior, is suggested by the research on 'forced-compliance' manipulations in the literature on cognitive dissonance. For instance, the series of studies reported by Nuttin (1975) provide many examples of people undertaking _appa-rently_ attitude-relevant behaviors for reasons _other than_ the wish to express their attitudes. There is still a possibility that the occurrence of attitude-discrepant behavior under such experimental conditions is interpretable as due to a strong bias influencing response tendency (e.g. if those whose initial attitudes were less extremely opposed showed such behavior more readily and more enthusiastically). However, the shifts in res-ponse tendency are typically so extreme that it seems more useful to interpret such manipulations as inducing subjects to view their behavior as not needing to be accounted for (at the time) as though it were expressive of their attitudes on the issue. As for the attitude change effects observed, these may be considered as dependent on subjects coming to see themselves as held accountable for such behavior after all.

The optimism expressed by judgment theorists concerning the substitutability of different response modalities (and hence concerning attitude-behavior consistency) needs therefore to be tempered by a consideration of how judgment experiments can differ from everyday life. By and large, in a judgment experi-ment, we know the stimuli to which our subjects are attending, and we know that our subjects are responding deliberately to express their representations of these stimuli. We are accustomed to cooperative subjects whose approach to the judgment task may often be to try to 'get it right'. Our subjects act as though they are being held accountable by the experimenter for the response they give.

Outside the laboratory things can be very different. People may attend and fail to attend to many disparate aspects of an uncontrolled environment. They may not be particularly concerned how their responses will be interpreted by others, or by whom they will be so interpreted. They may, as Langer (1978) puts it, often be reacting 'mindlessly' in a routine fashion, doing <u>and saying</u> whatever comes easiest.

Can we call behavior of this latter kind 'expressive' of the person's internal representations of relevant environmental stimuli? If we assume that all learnt behavior depends not just on the occurrence of stimuli, but on how such stimuli are represented in terms of expectancies, associations and so on, then in <u>some</u> sense it must be expressive. That is to say, such behavior 'expresses' internal representations of stimuli to the extent that we can infer something about these representations from observing the behavior. However, we do not need to assume either that such behavior is deliberately expressive, i.e. a deliberate attempt to <u>communicate</u> these internal representations to another person, or that such representations are necessarily available to introspection. Indeed, some authors argue that we typically have poor insight into the factors controlling our behavior (Nisbett and Wilson, 1977). Even if one avoids the debate over whether people can be influenced by stimuli of which they are unaware, there seem good grounds for supposing that people may have poor insight into the selectivity of their own interpretations of events. Hence, they may fail to recognize the idiosyncrasy of and their own judgmental frames of references in terms of which the consistency of their attitudes is defined and maintained.

We thus have a situation, on the one hand, where (e.g. conditioned) behavior that is not a deliberate attempt at communication may nonetheless communicate a good deal about a person's feelings about an attitude object, and, on the other hand, where even sincere and deliberate attempts at communication may not convey insightful information about the causes of the person's feelings and behavior. The apparent difficulty here is another product of the tendency to think of attitudes as causes rather than as meanings. It is the concept of meaning, rather than that of cause, that is vital to a definition of expressive behavior. We treat behavior as expressive to the extent that we think we can interpret its meaning, and we treat it as interpretable to the extent that we see it as consistent.

The situations under which we expect greater consistency are therefore the same as those under which we are more inclined to treat behavior as expressive of attitude. As I have argued, one way such consistency can arise is from the acquisition of contiguous responses to the same stimuli under the same conditions — i.e. from a common learning history. For example, Fazio and Zanna (1981) suggest that greater attitude—behavior consistency is to be expected when people's attitudes are based on direct experience of the issue or object in question. Their distinction between direct and indirect experience reflects differences in learning history.

Another route to consistency is through the imposition of social demands for predictability and accountability in terms of a given frame of reference. The literature on self—presentation (e.g. Schlenker, 1980) is replete with examples. So pervasive may be such demands that we may use them as criteria for self-evaluation. The attributes we see as relevant to ourselves tend also to be those where we see ourselves as more consistent (Bem and Allen, 1974). Any manipulations that allow for self-observation of a particular response modality, that is, that allow actors to view their behavior as it would appear to others, will therefore tend to increase the degree of actual or perceived consistency involving that modality. Bem's (1967) self-perception theory is relevant here, as are experimental studies by Storms (1970) and more recently, Roth and Upmeyer (1985).

In short, we tend to treat behavior as 'expressive' of attitude to the extent that we believe it to be consistent, and we tend to discount it to the extent that we believe it to be inconsistent. This is because what we do with the concept of attitude is to try and explain apparent consistencies in people's evaluative reactions to environmental events. However, when people appear inconsistent, we have great difficulty in applying the concept of attitude. This, though, may not be because their responses are any less sincere reflections of their internal representations, but because these internal representations may themselves be 'inconsistent' in terms of the frame of reference through which we view them.

It should follow also that anyone who deliberately wants to express their attitude should attempt to present their evaluative reactions as consistent. An inconsistent expression of attitude will be less easy to understand and hence be liable to be discounted. This has major methodological implications. Whenever someone fills in an attitude questionnaire, they almost certainly realize that their responses will be taken as expressive of their attitude. If we observe consistency in someone's questionnaire responses, then, could it be that such consistency has been artefactually inflated by the response task itself? This is a very real possibility, but how much it matters depends on the use to which such data will be put. If we want to use such data to tell us how people represent attitude objects when specifically directed to reflect upon them, there is no special problem. Consistency may be inflated, but this may be a product of the process of reflection and reconstruction itself (or if one prefers, that of communicating with oneself) rather than a ploy to please the researcher. On the other hand, if we wish to take such data as representative of nonreflective decision processes underlying ongoing behavior, in the absence of any demands to account for such decisions or communicate them to others, then there are strong grounds for caution.

How can one investigate such contextual pressures for consistency if all questionnaires contain them? One possibility (at least within the laboratory) is to take the speed of response to an attitude question as an index of the extent to which that attitude is well-formed and hence accessible. This was the approach taken by Fazio, Lenn and Effrein (1984), who observed shorter responses latencies under conditions when subjects had either completed a traditional attitude questionnaire, or had been instructed to expect that their preferences for different attitude objects could be functional for future behavior. Fazio et al. conclude that individuals may not necessarily form attitudes in any well-organized (and hence reportable) way unless they receive cues that it may be functional for them to reflect upon their own reactions.

Another approach is to vary the way in which the items in a questionnaire are presented so as to manipulate or disguise the frame of reference in terms of which subjects may expect their responses to be interpreted. An experiment by Budd (1987) provides an example. Subjects were required to complete measures of evaluative beliefs, subjective norms, motivation to comply, attitude and behavioral intention regarding three separate behavioral domains (smoking, exercising, brushing teeth) either with items relating to each domain presented in a separate section of the questionnaire in the order recommended by Ajzen and Fishbein (1980), or with items from all three domains randomly intermixed. Consistency — that is, in this context, the extent to which behavioral intention could be predicted from attitudes and subjective norms, and also the extent to which attitudes could be predicted from evaluative beliefs in accordance with the Fishbein and Ajzen (1975) model — was high when the three domains were kept separate but negligible when they were intermixed.

Is consistency, then, simply an artefact of the way that questions are asked? The answer I would give is that it is context-specific. Whether this amounts to it being an artefact depends on a value judgment of the ecological validity of the questioning technique we use, and the extent to which we feel it fairly simulates the elicitation of attitude-relevant responses in less contrived situations. The point more central to this paper though, is that whether real or artefactual, consistency has its main roots in interpersonal rather than intrapersonal processes.

X. Shared attitudes and social representations

The same conventional wisdom that urges us to think of attitudes as enduring structures 'inside the head' allows us also to talk of 'public opinion' as a mass noun and to expect a fair amount of consensus (though not unanimity) among different people's attitudes across a range of issues. But how can something as private as an attitude be shared, and aggregrated into something called 'public' opinion?

An implication of the argument presented here is that this question may be wrongly put — that the issue is not so much one of how something private and personal becomes public and social, but how something inherently social and public becomes interpreted as personal and private. Of course we feel and think, but the kinds of feelings and thoughts we call 'attitudes' are not 'things' but processes or events that we assume (a) are systematically related to actual or imagined events in the environment, and (b) can be expressed systematically in terms of a variety of more or less arbitrary response codes. In short, we assume a predictive relationship on the one hand between environmental events and their internal representations, and on the other hand between the internal representation of environmental events and various forms of expressive behavior.

How justified are we in our assumptions about such relationships? The answer is that it depends on which specific assumptions we are talking about. Any conception of attitude embodies some kind of psychological theory. A more naive psychological theory will produce a more naive conception of attitude. A less naive psychology theory, that is, one that incorporates or acknowledges more general psychological principles, may offer interpretations that sometimes challenge commonly held assumptions. One such assumption is that attitudes are naturally consistent with each other and with behavior.

I have relied extensively on three theoretical notions or principles, those of learning, accountability and judgment. From the principle of learning it can be expected that people will come to acquire common expectancies, affective and adaptive responses to environmental events to the extent that they share a common learning history with respect to such events. In other words, if they experience events within the same or similar contexts, they will come to represent and react to such events in the same or similar ways. There is thus no mystery, from a psychological point of view, why more uniform environmental circumstances within a society, more uniform public information, etc., should lead to more uniform forms of attitudinal response. What we are observing are the signs of a uniformity of learning history, of access to learning experiences, of political and familial socialization or whatever. What causes any such uniformity of learning history, though, is a question beyond the scope of any psychological theory of learning.

On the other hand, the same kind of principle that predicts that different individuals who share a common learning history should react in broadly similar ways to the same events, predicts that the responses of the same individual will differ to the extent that they are acquired in different contexts. I have argued that verbal statements of attitude may frequently be acquired more or less independently of other attitude-relevant responses. To the extent that this is so, inter-individual consensus at the level of verbal statements may reflect a shared learning history of how such verbal behavior has been acquired, but need not reflect shared personal experience with, or common internal representations of the attitude object to which such statements ostensibly refer.

As behaviors in their own right, statements of attitude may be acquired through processes of conditioning and imitation. To the extent that individuals are exposed to such statements in a stereotyped form, and on repeated occasions, these statements are likely to pass into the individuals' own behavioral repertoire. However, to say that particular statements (and individual stylistic variants) are so acquired is not to say that individuals have necessarily acquired the ability to reflect insightfully upon their own thoughts and feelings and express them meaningfully to others. Thus different people may make very similar kinds of statements on an issue, but we cannot necessarily assume that these reflect shared feelings or predispositions to react in other ways. A common verbal repertoire may disguise individual variation at the level of internal representation of events, even though it would typically be taken as an index of consensus both by those who hear and by those who make the statements.

The issue of how much consensus in thought one can infer from consensus in talk is of central relevance to the concept of social representations. According to Moscovici (1981, 1984) social psychology, particularly in its dominant anglophonic and North American tradition, has been excessively concerned with individual processes, and has paid far too little attention to the forms of thought that may be consensual among members of a particular society or social group. The proper study of attitudes from the point of view of the theory of social representations would therefore be the study of beliefs, values and ideologies that are so consensually accepted as not even to be recognizable as matters of opinion. As defined by Moscovici (1981 p. 186) "Social representations are phenomena that are linked with a special way of acquiring and communicating knowledge, a way that creates realities and common sense".

I have no quarrel with the plea for the psychological study of such consensual systems of beliefs and conceptions of reality. All scientific endeavor must take as its starting point a preparedness to question what is conventionally regarded as obviously true. However, many of the most important questions in attitude research are not easily considered in terms of such an approach in particular, the single most important question of all — that of why differences in attitude arise and persist.

This relates directly to one of the major ambiguities in the theory of social representations, the relationship between representation and language. It is a central assumption of the theory that representations acquire the status of consensual knowledge or common sense through communication. Language therefore is clearly essential for social representations, and indeed it is the use of conventional linguistic expressions among members of the same community or social group that is typically taken as evidence that such social representations exist (e.g. Hewstone,

1986). There is, however, a kind of circularity in asserting that social representations exist at the level of the social group, using language to define the content of such representations, and defining one's 'social group' as those sharing the same conventions of linguistic expression. Potter & Litton (1985) have proposed that a concept of 'linguistic repertoires' would be an improvement over that of social representations. They argue that Moscovici and others have failed to distinguish between the cognitive accessibility of the linguistic construct and the way that it is used in specific contexts.

It is certainly worth documenting the extent to which particular systems of values and conceptions of reality are widely shared within particular groups and communities. However, to assume that such forms of consensual thought constitute the psychological foundation of groups or cultures, ignores the fact that all communities and societies, if they are to adapt and survive in the face of change and in response to new information, must be able to express and synthesize potential <u>disagreement</u> as well as pre-existing consensus.

The appropriateness of any given linguistic construct as a way of describing some aspect of experienced reality, therefore, can in principle be a matter of debate. From this it follows that different individuals may use different linguistic forms to express similar experiences, or may use similar linguistic forms to express different experiences. This then brings us back to the questions of the criteria we use at an individual level, to infer what other people mean by what they say, and of the rules we learn to follow to insure (or render it more probable) that our own expressive behavior will be interpretable by others. This is where the notion of accountability comes into play.

XI. Accountability, judgment and consistency

Individuals learn that other people will form expectations of them on the basis of what they say and do, so that attitude-relevant behaviors become not simply responses but signs. We learn to control our attitude-relevant behaviors with a regard to how others will interpret them. We learn to think a little more about the meaning of the statements we make, so that our verbal expression of attitude becomes (we persuade ourselves) more reflective and less reactive. Above all, we learn that others expect us to be consistent between response modalities and within response modalities over time, and that unless such expectations are fulfilled, our expressive behavior will be regarded as uninterpretable or even dishonest. A tension is therefore set up between the learning of situation-specific responses to individual stimuli, and the acquisition of consistency in responses to stimulus categories across situations and across modalities. In many ways this parallels the debate beween situationist and trait approaches to personality (e.g. Bem and Allen, 1974; Mischel, 1968). However, whatever the origins of consistency in personality, consistency in attitude expression is according to my argument here, acquired as an accommodation to social demands.

THE EXPRESSION OF ATTITUDE

Whether such social demands would lead to more shared attitudes, is difficult to say, since in this case what is demanded relates primarily to the form of the relationships between attitude-relevant responses, rather than to the content of any response considered by itself. Nonetheless, such social demands could increase the conventionality or shared nature of people's attitude-relevant behavior by conveying the presumption that any conventionality people showed within one response modality would be predictive of a similar conventionality within other modalities also. When called to account for conventional affective reactions, for instance, people may generate more conventional verbal statements and interpersonal behavior. However, it is likely to be precisely those individual responses that are most conventional or widely shared for which an actor is least likely to be held to account (Jones and Davis, 1965; Langer, 1978). Conventionality can be present without consistency.

Consistency, though, is itself relative to the selective frame of reference in terms of which the attitude objects are evaluated. This is where notions of judgment assume importance. On the one hand, any response modality can be regarded as expressive of a person's internal representations of an attitude object. On the other hand, any such representation, and any expression of it, will concentrate upon the more salient attributes or dimensions of the object being judged. How do individuals come to select certain attributes as salient? Consistency with a positive self-evaluation is a useful predictor (Eiser and Mower White, 1974), with individuals treating as most salient those dimensions in terms of which they can attach evaluatively positive labels to items of which they approve. People who take up different standpoints on an issue tend to express, and indeed account for, their attitudes in terms of different kinds of value-laden language.

Although language provides us with a wide choice of ways to express our attitudes, in practice there are social constraints on such choice. We learn what dimensions of description are likely to be acceptable in different social contexts when expressing our viewpoints on a given issue. We acquire, that is, a shared linguistic style for expressing particular attitudes, reflecting at least partly a shared selectivity in the aspects of the issue to be regarded as salient. Since language is our prime means of communication, it is also the prime route through which attitudes may come to be shared. Language, too, provides us with concepts and sets of categories in terms of which events can be evaluated and represented.

What this means is that any normative social influences on the kind of value-laden language people will apply to a particular issue could lead to more shared attitudes, over and above direct influences to adopt one particular position rather than another. If such language is used reflectively, it can (a) imply that some positions are more easy to justify or account for than others; and (b) help define the selective frames of reference in terms of which given attitudinal representations appear consistent or inconsistent.

We can therefore expect attitudes, in the sense of internal representations to be shared to the extent (a) that people are exposed to similar information about the environment; and (b) that such information is encoded in terms of similar categories, schemata or frames of reference. We can expect attitude-relevant responses to be shared to the extent that people acquire specific behaviors under common environmental conditions, to the extent that such behaviors are acquired through imitation, and to the extent that more conventional responses, whether verbal or non-verbal are more likely to be reinforced by others. The main difficulty though, remains that of knowing how far shared responses reflect shared internal representations.

When we talk of attitudes being 'shared', we are assuming that people share the same (or similar) internal representations of environmental events. But we can, of course, never know this for sure. All we have to go on is correspondence between the attitude-relevant _responses_ shown by different individuals. Up to a point, this is no different from the conceptual problems faced in many other fields of psychology, where we infer latent psychological processes from overt behavior. The special problem with regard to attitudes is that the meaning we attribute to such responses depends on further assumptions we make about the extent to which they are truly expressive of such _internal_ representations, rather than conditioned to, or 'manded' (cf. Fazio, Herr, and Olney, 1984) by features of the _external_ situation. Among the most important situational features that might affect the form of such responses are the presence of other people, and their anticipated reactions. Such influences will presumably tend to act in the direction of producing greater conformity of response. We thus face a basic dilemma: shared attitudes need to be inferred from shared or conventional expressive responses, but the more conventional such responses are, the more reason there seems to be to doubt whether such responses really are 'expressive' of internal representations, rather than indicative of social pressure at the level of response.

One should therefore be cautious of extrapolating from observation of a conventional _response_ within one modality to a prediction of conventional responses in other modalities, or to an inference of consensus at the level of internal representation. If people can respond in similar ways without 'really thinking', we cannot assume that they are necessarily having similar thoughts when their responses are similar.

XII. Attitude as a social product

Much work in attitude theory appears to start from the assumption that attitudes are or should be coherently organized wholes, and it then proceeds to try and explain why, despite this, one observes inconsistency at the level of response. I have argued for a reverse position — that many of the responses that we treat as relevant to a particular attitude have separate learning histories and may be elicited by separate environmental stimuli. The basic question is not how they come to be rather independent of each other, but how they come to be interpreted as interdependent and related to each other. To understand how attitudes are acquired we must address the question both of how we acquire sets of attitude-relevant responses, and of how we acquire the capacity to reflect upon such responses and control them so that they seem meaningful to others and to ourselves. Without such a reflective capacity, attitudes cannot be thought of as organized representations of events.

The question of how we interpret our own and others' behavior is bound up with the notion of consistency. Inconsistent information about a person seems to elicit more active processing, and more attempts to reinterpret events and revise existing schemata (Crocker, Fiske and Taylor, 1984; Stern, Marrs, Millar and Cole, 1984) whereas consistency in an individuals' attitude-relevant responses seems to be accepted as a criterion for infering the strength (Chaiken and Baldwin, 1981; Norman, 1975) and sincerity (Budd, 1983; Smith, 1982) of expressed attitudes. However, consistency, at least among responses elicited under different stimulus conditions, is itself a _social_ product, and a response to demands for accountability and apparent rationality that (however much they may become internalized through socialization) are _interpersonal_ in origin.

Consistency is not a natural state toward which all our thoughts and feelings aspire. It is something achieved through selectivity and bias, but with such selectivity and bias we can buy simplicity. With the simplicity so bought, we can communicate, and so potentially modify our environment. But is this simplicity a true summary or a distortion? Ultimately, there may be no way of really telling. Introspection may be a less than reliable guide, for we may have little insight into how we have been selective in our thoughts, so consistency may not be a valid criterion for the 'truth' of our expression of attitude.

But if we abandon our reliance on consistency, what are we left with? The answer is possibly a pandemonium of separate affective and instrumental response tendencies to specific stimuli embedded in specific contexts, associated with separate expectancies and beliefs. Would such a pandemonium constitute an attitude? In a sense, one could say, yes, why not? The trouble, though, is that whilst we could choose to _define_ this pandemonium as an attitude, we could not actually _describe_ it as such. The language of attitudinal description demands at least a modicum of consistency based either on affective cognitive and behavioral responses to the _same_ stimuli being acquired together, or on the feasibility of grouping _different_ stimuli and responses into categories.

It is very difficult to describe psychological processes as 'attitudinal', or behavior as expressive of 'attitude', without assuming some degree of generalizability across contexts and/or modalities. Whether such assumptions are correct in general is no longer critical. The point is that when we _can_ assume such generalizability, we can bring the concept of attitude into play. However an attitude is not something _other than_ such processes and behavior. It is a concept we use to interpret and communicate our representations of events. Such interpretation and communication requires a degree of cross-situational consistency, but such consistency, I have argued, is a social product. Were it not for the social demands that our responses to the environment be predictable and communicable, we would have little or no need for the concept of attitude. If we reserve the concept of attitude for those representations and responses that reflect such demands, then an attitude, too, is a social product.

REFERENCES

Abelson, R.P., Aronson, E., McGuire, W.J., Newcomb, T.M., Rosenberg, M.J. & Tannenbaum, P.H. (Eds.), Theories of cognitive consistency: A sourcebook. Chicago: Rand McNally, 1968.

Ajzen, I. & Fishbein, M. Understanding attitudes and predicting social behavior. Englewood Cliffs, N.J.: Prentice-Hall, 1980.

Allport, G.W. Attitudes. In C. Murchison (Ed.), A handbook of social psychology. Worcester, Mass: Clark University Press, 1935.

Anderson, N.H. On the role of context effects in psychophysical judgement. Psychological Review. 1975, 82, 462–482.

Anderson, N.H. Equity judgments as information integration. Journal of Personality and Social Psychology. 1976, 33, 291–299.

Anscombe, G.E.M. Intention. Oxford: Blackwell, 1963 (2nd Edition).

Baumeister, R.F. A self-presentational view of social phenomena Psychological Bulletin, 1982, 91, 3–26.

Bem, D.J. Self-perception: An alternative interpretation of cognitive dissonance phenomena. Psychological Review, 1967, 47 183–200.

Bem, D.J. & Allen, A. On predicting some of the people some of the time: The search for cross-situational consistencies in behavior. Psychological Review, 1974, 81, 506–520.

Billig, M. Prejudice, categorization and particularization: From a perceptual to a rhetorical approach. European Journal of Social Psychology, 1985, 15, 79–103.

Bower, G. Prime time in cognitive psychology. Paper presented to the 14th Annual Congress of the European Association for Behaviour Therapy. Brussels, September 1984.

REFERENCES

Breckler, S. J. Validation of affect, behavior and cognition as distinct components of attitude. Unpublished doctoral dissertation, Ohio State University, Columbus, 1983.

Breckler, S.J. Empirical validation of affect, behavior and cognition as distinct components of attitude. Journal of Personality and Social Psychology, 47, 1191-1205.

Budd, R.J. A critique of Fishbein's theory of reasoned action: Exemplified by findings from the domain of social drug-use. Unpublished Ph.D. Dissertation. University of Sheffield, 1983.

Budd, R.J. Response bias in the theory of reasoned action. Social Cognition, 1987 (in press).

Chaiken, S. & Baldwin, M.W. Affective-cognitive consistency and the effect of salient behavioral information on the self-perception of attitudes. Journal of Personality and Social Psychology, 1981,41, 1-12.

Chomsky, N. Review of 'Verbal Behavior' by B.F. Skinner. Language. 1959, 35, 26-58.

Clark, M.S. & Fiske, S.T. (Eds.), Affect and cognition:The 17th Annual Carnegie Symposium on Cognition. Hillsdale, N.J.: Erlbaum, 1982.

Coombs, C.H. A theory of data. New York: Wiley, 1964.

Cooper, J. & Fazio, R.H. A new look at dissonance theory. In L. Berkowitz (Ed.), Advances in Experimental Social Psychology Vol. 17, New York: Academic Press, 1984.

Cooper, J., Zanna, M.P. & Taves, P.A. Arousal as a necessary condition for attitude change following compliance. Journal of Personality and Social Psychology, 1978, 36, 1101-1106.

Crocker, J., Fiske, S.T. & Taylor, S.E. Schematic bases of belief change. In J.R. Eiser (Ed.), Attitudinal Judgement, New York: Springer-Verlag, 1984.

Eiser, J.R. Categorization, cognitive consistency, and the concept of dimensional salience. European Journal of Social Psychology, 1971, 1, 435-454.

Eiser, J.R. Attitudes and the use of evaluative language:A two-way process. Journal for the Theory of Social Behaviour. 1975, 5, 235-248.

Eiser, J. R. Cognitive social psychology: A guidebook to theory and research. London: McGraw-Hill, 1980.

Eiser, J.R. Attitudinal Judgement. New York: Springer-Verlag, 1984.

Eiser, J. R. Social psychology: Attitudes, cognition and social behaviour. Cambridge: Cambridge University Press, 1986.

REFERENCES

Eiser, J.R. & Mower White, C.J. Evaluative consistency and social judgment. <u>Journal of Personality and Social Psychology</u>. 1974, <u>30</u>, 349–359.

Eiser, J.R. & Mower White, C.J. Categorization and congruity in attitudinal judgment. <u>Journal of Personality and Social Psychology</u>. 1975, <u>31</u>, 769–775.

Eiser, J.R. & Pancer, S.M. Attitudinal effects of the use of evaluatively biased language. <u>European Journal of Social Psychology</u>. 1979, <u>9</u>, 39–47.

Eiser, J.R. & Ross, M. Partisan language, immediacy, and attitude change. <u>European Journal of Social Psychology</u>. 1977, <u>7</u>, 477–489.

Eiser, J.R. & Stroebe, W. <u>Categorization and Social Judgement</u>. London: Academic Press, 1972.

Eiser, J.R. & van der Pligt, J. Accentuation and perspective in attitudinal judgment. <u>Journal of Personality and Social Psychology</u>, 1982, <u>42</u>, 224–238.

Eiser, J.R. & van der Pligt, J. Accentuation theory, polarization, and the judgment of attitude statements. In J.R. Eiser (Ed.), <u>Attitudinal Judgment</u>. New York: Springer Verlag, 1984.

Fazio, R.H. How do attitudes guide behavior? In R.M. Sorrentino & E. T. Higgins (Eds.), <u>The Handbook of Motivation and Cognition: Foundations of Social Behavior</u>. New York: Guilford Press, 1986.

Fazio, R.H., Herr, P.M. & Olney, T.J. Attitude accessibility following a self-perception process. <u>Journal of Personality and Social Psychology</u>, 1984, <u>47</u>, 277–286.

Fazio, R. H., Lenn, T.M. & Effrein, E.A. Spontaneous attitude formation. <u>Social Cognition</u>, 1984, 217–234.

Fazio, R.H., Powell, M.C. & Herr, P.M. Toward a process model of the attitude-behavior relation: Accessing one's attitude upon more observation of the attitude object. <u>Journal of Personality and Social Psychology</u>, 1983, <u>44</u>, 723–735.

Fazio, R.H. & Zanna, M.P. Direct exerience and attitude behavior consistency. In L. Berkowitz (Ed.), <u>Advances in Experimental Social Psychology</u>, (Vol. 14. New York: Academic Press, 1981.

Fazio, R.H., Zanna, M.P. & Cooper, J. Dissonance and self-perception: An integrative view of each theory's proper domain of application. <u>Journal of Experimental Social Psychology</u>, 1977, <u>13</u>, 464–479.

Festinger, L. <u>A theory of cognitive dissonance</u>. Evanston, Ill.: Row, Peterson, 1957.

REFERENCES

Fishbein, M. & Ajzen, I. Belief, attitude intention and behavior: An introduction to theory and research. Reading Mass. : Addison—Wesley, 1975.

Ginsburg, G. P., Brenner, M. & von Cranach, M. Discovery strategies in the psychology of action. London: Academic Press, 1985.

Gollob, H.F. The subject—verb—object approach to social cognition. Psychological Review, 1974, 81, 286—321.

Greenwald, A.G. On defining attitude and attitude theory. In A.G. Greenwald, T.C. Brock and T.M. Ostrom (Eds). Psychological foundations of attitudes. New York : Academic Press, 1968.

Harre, R. & Secord, P.F. The explanation of social behaviour. Oxford: Blackwell, 1972.

Heider, F. Attitudes and cognitive organization. Journal of Psychology, 1946, 21, 107—112.

Heider, F. The psychology of interpersonal relations. New York: Wiley, 1958.

Herrnstein, R.J. Relative and absolute strength of response as a function of frequency of reinforcement. Journal of the Experimental Analysis of Behavior, 1961, 4, 267—274.

Hewstone, M. Understanding attitudes to the European Community A social psychological study in four member states. Cambridge: Cambridge University Press, 1986.

Higgins, E.T. & Lurie, L. Context categorization, and recall: The "change—of—standard" effect. Cognitive Psychology, 1983, 15, 525—547.

Higgins, E.T., Rholes, W.S. & Jones, C.R. Category accessibility and impression formation. Journal of Experimental Social Psychology, 1977, 13, 141—154.

James, W. Psychology : The briefer course. New York: Holt 1910.

Jaspars, J.M.F. On social perception. Unpublished Ph.D. Thesis. University of Leiden, 1965.

Jones, E.E. & Davis, K.E. From acts to dispositions: The attribution process in person perception. In L. Berkowitz (Ed.) Advances in Experimental Social Psychology, Vol. 2. New York: Academic Press, 1965.

Kamin, L. J. Predictability, surprise, attention and conditioning. In B.A. Campbell & R.M. Church (Eds.), Punishment and and Aversive Behavior. New York: Appleton—Century—Crofts, 1969.

Kelly, H.H. & Michela, J.L. Attribution theory and research. Annual Review of Psychology, 1980, 31, 457—501.

REFERENCES

Kothandapani, V. Validation of feeling, belief and intention to act as three components of attitude and their contribution to prediction of contraceptive behavior. <u>Journal of Personality and Social Psychology</u>, 1971, <u>19</u>, 321–333.

Kristiansen, C.M. Value correlates of preventive health behavior. <u>Journal of Personality and Social Psychology</u>, 1985 <u>49</u>, 748–758.

Langer, E. J. Rethinking the role of thought in social inter-action. In J.H. Harvey, W.J. Ickes & R.F. Kidd (Eds.), <u>New Directions in Attribution Research</u>, Vol. 2, Hillsdale, N.J.: Erlbaum, 1978, pp. 35–58.

Langford, G. Persons as necessarily social. <u>Journal for the Theory of Social Behaviour</u>, 1978,<u>8</u>, 263–283.

Martin, L.K. & Riess, D. Effects of US intensity during previous discrete delay conditioning on conditioned acceleration during avoidance extinction. <u>Journal of Comparative and Physiological Psychology</u>, 1969, <u>69</u>, 196–200.

McDougall, W. <u>An introduction to social psychology</u>. London : London : Methuen, 1908.

Moscovici, S. On social representation. In J.P. Forgas (Ed.) <u>Social cognition: Perspectives on everyday understanding</u>, London: Academic Press, 1981, pp. 181–209.

Moscovici, S. The phenomenon of social representations. In R.M. Farr and S. Moscovici (Eds.) <u>Social Representations</u>, Cambridge: Cambridge University Press, 1984, pp. 3–69.

Nisbett, R. E. & Ross, L. <u>Human Inference : Strategies and shortcomings of social judgement</u>. Englewood Cliffs, N.J. : Prentice-Hall, 1980.

Nisbett, R.E. & Wilson, T.D. Telling more than we can know: Verbal reports on mental processes. <u>Psychological Review</u>, 1977, <u>84</u>, 231–259.

Norman, R. Affective–cognitive consistency, attitudes, con-formity and behavior. <u>Journal of Personality and Social Psychology</u>, 1975, <u>32</u>, 83–91.

Nowell–Smith, P.H. <u>Ethics.</u> Hammondsworth, Penguin, 1956.

Nuttin, J.M., Jr. <u>The illusion of attitude change: Towards a a response contagion theory of persuasion.</u> London: Academic Press, 1975.

Osgood, C.E. & Tannenbaum, P.H. The principle of congruity in the prediction of attitude change. <u>Psychological Review</u>, 1955, <u>62</u>, 42–55.

Ostrom, T. M. The relationship between the affective, behavioral and cognitive components of attitude. <u>Journal of Experimental Social Psychology</u>, 1969, <u>5</u>, 12–30.

Parducci, A. Range-frequency compromise in judgement. Psychological Monographs, 1963, 77, (2, Whole No. 565).

Petty, R.E. & Cacioppo, J.T. The elaboration likelihood model of persuasion. In L. Berkowitz (Ed.), Advances in experimental social psychology. Vol. 19, New York: Academic Press, 1985.

Potter, J. & Litton, I. Some problems underlying the theory of social representations. British Journal of Social Psychology, 1985, 24, 81-90.

Rescorla, R.S. Probability of shock in the presence and absence of CS in fear conditioning. Journal of Comparative and Physiological Psychology, 1968, 66, 1-5.

Rescorla, R.A. Variations in the effectiveness of reinforcement and nonreinforcement following prior inhibitory condition-ing. Learning and Motivation, 1971, 2, 113-123.

Rescorla, R.S. & Solomon, R.L. Two-process learning theory: Relationships between Pavlovian conditioning and instru-mental learning. Psychological Review, 1967, 74, 151-182.

Rokeach, M. Value survey. Sunnyvale, CA : Halgren Tests 1967.

Rokeach, M. Understanding human values: Individual and societal New York: Free Press, 1979.

Ross, L. The intuitive psychologist and his shortcomings: Distortions in the attribution process. In L. Berkowitz, (Ed.), Advances in Experimental Social Psychology, New York New York: Academic Press, 1977.

Rosenberg, M. J. & Hovland, C. I. Cognitive, affective and behavioral components of attitudes. In M.J. Rosenberg, C.I. Hovland, W.J. McGuire, R. P. Ableson & J. W. Brehm (Eds.), Attitude organization and change: An analysis of consistency among attitude components. Hew Haven, Conn.: Yale University Press, 1960.

Roth, H.G. & Upmeyer, A. Matching attitudes towards cartoons across evaluative judgments and nonverbal evaluative behavior. Psychological Research, 1985, 47, 173-183.

Schank, R.C. & Abelson, R.P. Scripts, plans, goals, and under-standing: An enquiry into human knowledge. Hillsdale, N.J.: Erlbaum, 1977.

Schlenker, B.R. Impression management: The self concept, social identity, and interpersonal relations. Montrey, Calif. : Brooks/Cole, 1980.

Schlenker, B.R. Translating actions into attitudes: An identity-analytic approach to the explanation of social conduct. In L. Berkowitz (Ed.) Advances in Experimental Social Psychology, Vol. 15, New York: Academic Press, 1982.

Smith, J.L. A structuralist interpretation of the Fishbein model of behavioral intentions. Journal of the Theory of Social Behavior, 1982, 12, 29-46.

REFERENCES

Stern, L.D., Marrs, S., Millar, M.G. & Cole, E. Processing time and the recall of inconsistent and consistent behaviors of individuals and groups. Journal of Personality and Social Psychology, 1984, 47, 253-262.

Stevens, S.S. Adaptation-level versus the relativity of judgement. American Journal of Psychology, 1958, 71, 633-646.

Storms, M.D. Videotape and the attribution process: Reversing actors' and observers' points of view. Journal of Personality and Social Psychology, 1973, 27, 165-175.

Streufert, S. & Streufert, S. C. Behavior in the complex environment. Washington, D.C.: Winston, 1978.

Tajfel, H. Quantitative judgement in social perception. British Journal of Psychology, 1959, 50, 16-29.

Tarpy, R. M. Principles of animal learning and motivation. Glenview, Ill.: Scott, Foresman, 1982.

Taylor, S.E. & Fiske, S.T. Salience, attention and attribution: Top of the head phenomena. In L. Berkowitz (Ed.), Advances in Experimental Social Psychology. Vol. 11, New York: Academic Press, 1978.

Taylor, S. E., Fiske, S. T., Etcoff, N. L. & Roderman, A.J. Categorical and contextual bases of person memory and stereotyping. Journal of Personality and Social Psychology. 1978, 36, 778-793.

Tedeschi, J.T. & Rosenfeld, P. Impression management theory and the forced compliance situation. In J.T. Tedeschi (Ed.), Impression management theory and social psychological research. New York: Academic Press, 1981.

Tedeschi, J.T., Schlenker, B.R. & Bonoma, T.V. Cognitive dissonance : Private ratiocination or public spectacle? American Psychologist, 1971, 26, 685-695.

Tetlock, P.E. & Manstead, A.S.R. Impression management versus intrapsychic explanations in social psychology: A useful dichotomy? Psychological Review, 1985, 92, 59-77.

Thurstone, L.L. Attitudes can be measured. American Journal of Sociology, 1928, 33, 529-554.

Upmeyer, A. Perceptual and judgmental processes in social contexts. In L. Berkowitz (Ed.), Advances in Experimental Social Psychology, Vol.14, New York: Academic Press, 1981.

Upshaw, H.S. The personal reference scale: An approach to social judgment. In L. Berkowitz (Ed.), Advances in Experimental Social Psychology, Vol. 4, New York: Academic Press, 1969.

Upshaw, H.S. Social influence on attitudes and on anchoring of congeneric attitudes scales. Journal of Experimental Social Psychology, 1978, 14, 327-339.

REFERENCES

Upshaw, H.S. & Ostrom, T.M. Psychological perspective in attitude research. In J.R. Eiser (Ed.), <u>Attitudinal judgment</u>. New York: Springer—Verlag, 1984.

Upshaw, H.S., Ostrom, T. M. & Ward, C.D. Content versus self-rating in attitude research. <u>Journal of Experimental Social Psychology</u>, 1970, <u>6</u>, 272—279.

van der Pligt, J. & Eiser, J.R. Dimensional salience, judgment, and attitudes. In J.R. Eiser (Ed.), <u>Attitudinal Judgement</u>. New York: Springer—Verlag, 1984.

van der Pligt, J. & van Dijk, J.A. Polarization of judgment and preference for judgmental labels. <u>European Journal of Social Psychology</u>, 1979, <u>9</u>, 233—242.

von Cranach, M., Kalbermatten, U., Indermuhle, K. & Gugler, B. <u>Goal—directed action</u>. London: Academic Press, 1982.

Wicker, A.W. Attitudes versus actions: The relationship of overt behavioral responses to attitude objects. <u>Journal of Social Psychology</u>, 1969, <u>25</u>, 41—78.